Please renew/return this item by the last date shown.

So that your telephone call is charged at local rate,
please call the numbers as set out below:

	From Area codes 01923 or 0208:	From the rest of Herts:
Renewals:	01923 471373	01438 737373
Enquiries:	01923 471333	01438 737333
Minicom:	01923 471599	01438 737599

L32b

J. B. Priestley

J. B. Priestley by David Hockney, 1973

J. B. Priestley

JOHN BRAINE

Weidenfeld and Nicolson · London

First published in Great Britain by
Weidenfeld & Nicolson Ltd
91 Clapham High Street London sw4
1978

ISBN 0 297 77505 7

Printed in Great Britain by
Butler & Tanner Ltd, Frome and London

Contents

Illustrations

Acknowledgements

My thanks are due to Canon John Collins and Diana Collins, Norman Collins, Judi Dench, Iris Murdoch, Colin Wilson and Ion Trewin, and, above all, to J. B. Priestley and Jacquetta Hawkes for giving so generously of their time. I am also grateful to A. D. Peters & Co. Ltd and William Heinemann Ltd for permission to quote copyright material from the works of J. B. Priestley.

I would also like to acknowledge the following people and organizations for kind permission to reproduce illustrations: Kasmin Ltd on behalf of David Hockney, and Bradford Art Galleries and Museums, for the frontispiece; Mander & Mitchenson, endpaper cartoon, 9, 10, 12, 14, 18, 19, 28 and 29; Radio Times Hulton Picture Library, 3, 8, 13, 15, 16, 20, 23, 24 and 25; Bradford Telegraph and Argus, 1; Bradford Central Library, 2 and 6; Clive Coote (Photographer), 4; Mrs M. Bruce, Bradford, 5; Ilkley Library, 7; Zoë Dominic, 11; National Film Archive, 17, 21, 26 and 30; Angus McBean Photograph, Harvard Theatre Collection, 22; Mark Gerson and John Vickers, 27; Lord Snowdon and Camera Press, 31 and 32; Fox Photos, 33. Picture research by Annette Brown.

Foreword

This book is in no sense a critical analysis of the work of J. B. Priestley.
And it is necessarily selective, in view of his enormous output. (As
the writer of a book about him I have cursed him as many times
for his fecundity as I have blessed him for it as a reader.) Naturally
I value some of his works more highly than others; but it does not
follow from this that what I don't mention I consider to have no
value.

My most important qualification to write this book is that since
the age of five reading has been my chief pleasure. I emphasize the
word pleasure; though enlightenment has often come along with
the pleasure. I have never read primarily to improve my mind. A
man may want a son; but he doesn't think of babies when he's begetting
him. I write about Priestley quite simply because I have always found
him supremely readable and, I should add, as a playwright supremely
watchable – for want of a better word.

A second qualification is that, to use Priestley's words in *Literature
and Western Man*, I speak as one whose experience has taken me out
of the dining-room where many critics and most literary historians
may be found, into the kitchen where the dinners are cooked. I speak
as a professional novelist who has made occasional ventures into TV
drama and even unsuccessful ventures into the theatre. As a reader
I have enjoyed myself in the best seats in the arena, sipping my old
Falnerian in the shade, a connoisseur and an addict. As a writer I
know what it's like down there in the blood and sand. I may not
have fought as long as Priestley or have won so many fights, but
I have survived. I am a professional.

I

The third qualification is our common background. I was born in a street less than two miles away from the street where he was born, and off the same road. The Bradford in which he grew up was, outwardly at least, the Bradford in which I grew up. The countryside around Bradford was the same. Above all, the moors were the same. And although something went out of it during the First World War, never to return, it was still a city with a character of its own, with its own traditions; not a beautiful city, but a *nourishing* city, a city to love. It has been almost wholly destroyed now and the destruction, the slow murder of a great city, began with the demolition of the Swan Arcade, where in 1911 Priestley went to work with Helm and Company, a small wool firm, after leaving Belle Vue Grammar School.

J. B. Priestley came to Bradford to make a TV programme about the demolition and his memories of the Swan Arcade, and that was the occasion of our first meeting. The excitement I felt then is still with me. From the age of fifteen, when I first read *The Good Companions*, I had felt closer to him than to any other living writer. I had read virtually everything he'd written and, thanks to the Bradford Civic Playhouse, had seen some of his most important plays, notably *Johnson Over Jordan*. I had grown up with him, he was part of my life, he was, so to speak, one of the family. My mother had changed his books for him at Bradford Central Library in Darley Street where, at the time of our meeting, a large oil painting of him still hung. I had learned a great deal from him, though not, as I came to realize later, as much as I could have learned. Above all, his example had encouraged me at those moments in my youth when I'd felt totally isolated in a world which had no room for writers. Priestley's background and mine were far from being identical. But there were sufficient resemblances to convince me that if he'd done it, so could I. It wouldn't have been possible for me to connect in the same way with a writer like, for instance, Aldous Huxley or Graham Greene or Christopher Isherwood. It wasn't that I didn't admire them, it wasn't that I felt the least hostility towards them; it was simply that they came from a totally different world, were almost a different species. There could be no identification of myself with anyone from a Home Counties bourgeois family who went straight to Oxbridge from Eton and from there into a world where somehow or other one always knew the right people.

Priestley understood all this without bitterness. He understood, too, what it's like to be entirely dependent upon one's own efforts and understood not only the fierce pride and independence which this generates but the moments of despair and the grinding fatigue. Apart from this he stood for the spirit best expressed in his father's words: *If you have more, you must give more.* I didn't think that he was a saint or that he couldn't make mistakes. But the values which he stood for were values which I could accept. It was difficult to put them into words because the politicians had twisted all the words for their own ends. And not only the politicians: what was being done to the Swan Arcade, for instance, was nominally supposed to make Bradford a better city to live in. Its real purpose was prestige for the politicians, profit for the developers, and jobs for the bureaucrats. It wouldn't make life better for the citizens of Bradford, but worse, spreading remorselessly over the whole city, a tumour of glass and steel and concrete and plastic, creating areas totally unfit for human beings to live in, districts which made the worst of the old slums seem like paradise.

Priestley understood this, and much more. He had a vision of a just society, a civilized and harmonious whole, a society in which there would be no alienation. He wanted a society in which diversity would flourish, in which individuality would be cherished, but also a society where the guiding principle would be that we can't live for ourselves alone, that we depend upon each other. He thought it monstrous that one section of the people should live in clean and pleasant places and another, and the larger, in dirty and hideous places. He thought it even more monstrous that, by and large, the most reliable way to be rich, to live in a clean and pleasant place, should be not to actually make anything useful or beautiful or to perform any essential service but merely to manipulate pieces of paper.

I never saw him as a doctrinaire socialist. I didn't really see him as a political animal at all. I saw him as one who would consider each issue independently and not according to how neatly it could be accommodated within the framework of an ideology. I saw him

3

as having a deep and genuine love for his country but none at all for the State. I saw him, above all, as someone I could look up to, someone who was unquestionably superior to myself. I saw him, in his own phrase, as a life-enhancer. I saw him as one of the few figures of our time with genuine glamour. It wasn't show-business glamour. It was the glamour of the great creative artist; it was not so much a question of what he was but what he had made. Waiting to meet him for lunch at the old Alexander Hotel in Great Horton Road I tried to find an image which would represent what he meant to me. What came to me was experienced rather than felt. There was a picture in my mind of being lost on a dark cold night and seeing the big house on the hill with light at all its windows and the sound of music as I came nearer, and there was the assurance that inside the big house there was food and warmth and I'd hear the music plainly.

There was something else: it wasn't I who saw the big house on the hill but *we*. He was, whilst being wholly and passionately English, an international figure. He wasn't, anywhere in the world, the *English* writer, J. B. Priestley, but simply J. B. Priestley. And when one was, to use Arnold Bennett's words coming out of a Toscanini concert, *given a lift* by his work, that lift was shared all over the world, one was part of a crowd in the proper way, a volunteer not a conscript, barriers were being broken down, there was the hope that the world might be made a better place.

My first meeting with him was a happy one, as all my subsequent meetings have been. I found no dissonance of public face and private face, no dissonance of the man and his work. In only one respect was he different from the man whose face I'd seen so often in photographs and sometimes on TV. In three dimensions, seen directly with the human eye, his face had a curious youthfulness. It was a lived-in face of great force, its owner never having the time to worry about what impression it gave. But it wasn't, somehow, old. It still isn't old. It never will be. I believe that this curious youthfulness – about which the camera always lies – is the gift conferred upon all those who use to the fullest the talents which they are given, who live for something outside themselves.

I have always remembered the excitement of first meeting Priestley and the astounding comfort it gave me to say that I was honoured and delighted to meet him, and to mean every word of it. I have experienced that excitement in writing about his work and I can only hope that I communicate it.

1

The Apprentice Sorcerer

The most important fact to bear in mind about John Boynton Priestley is that he was born privileged – more privileged, perhaps, than any other writer of his era. It is rather as if the life force had deliberately decided to create a hugely talented writer, one who would use his talents to the utmost and yet remain a sane and balanced human being, their servant and not their victim.

His three great privileges were that he was born of the right parents at the right time in the right place. This is the total of his inheritance and this is the source of his enormous strength. This is all that he was given. There never was any possibility of a family fortune, there were no family connections to ease his way. Those three privileges were absolutely his only privileges, absolutely all that he was given. Whatever he has achieved, he has achieved entirely through his own efforts. Indeed, he has worked for his living ever since leaving Belle Vue Grammar School, Bradford, at the age of seventeen. Whatever money he possesses – and if he had not chosen to live in England he would be a very rich man – he has earned through hard and honest work. Even at difficult periods of his life he has never borrowed. And this is relevant to any study of his work. It means that he has always been his own man. It means that he has always written only what he himself wanted to write. To be under an obligation to anyone – even, for instance, the most enlightened of publishers – is to diminish one's freedom, to speak with someone else's voice rather than one's own.

The ability to be a creative writer is of course something one is born with, the consequence of a particular genetic mix. There has to be a combination of intense sensitivity, of an unceasing and trans-forming inward force, and an ordering intelligence. That is, ordering not in the sense of originating the orders, but of giving order to the inward force, of making channels for it, of imposing a pattern. Inescapably this is an over-simplification. The delight of creative writing – and delight is as inseparable an element of it as it is of sex – is as much in making the pattern as it is in being taken over by the inward force. But it is all making, making and growing. There must be emotional vitality and, equally, there must be intellectual stamina.

Priestley was born in 1894 at 34 Mannheim Road, Toller Lane, Bradford. Mannheim Road still stands, a street of small stone terrace houses. Toller Lane begins as Westgate in the city centre. Westgate runs through what was formerly a working-class quarter, predominantly Irish, its focus point St Patrick's Church, which was built in the middle of the last century to serve the influx of Irish immigrants who came as a consequence of the famine. (It is relevant to note that the descendants of those immigrants began to move out after the Second World War, to be replaced by Displaced Persons from Eastern Europe and the Baltic States, and that the Displaced Persons began to move out in the Fifties to be replaced by Pakistanis.) The road begins to climb when it becomes Toller Lane, both in terms of height above sea-level and socially. Nearer the top of the hill is 5 Saltburn Place, where the family moved to in 1904. There is a description of it in Priestley's *The Edwardians*:

> It had a kitchen, where we ate when we were by ourselves; a front-room, where we ate when we had company; a smaller and gloomier back room … a bathroom on the half-landing, two bedrooms and two attics … The front attic was my bedroom from the first, and afterwards … my 'den'. This house, solidly built of stone, cost about £550.

Very roughly speaking, lower down, the district was working class and Catholic and further up the hill middle-class and Methodist.

Priestley's father, Jonathan Priestley, was a schoolmaster. He taught for some years at Belle Vue Grammar School, Bradford, and then was appointed head to the senior school of a big new elementary school at Green Lane (which is neither green nor a lane but a long black road). His salary was about £350, a comfortable middle-class income at a time when the median working-class wage was twenty-five shillings a week, and thirty shillings bought a made-to-measure suit, and tuppence bought a pint of strong beer.

He and his father, a mill worker who probably earned about thirty shillings a week, together performed some little miracle of thrift so that he was able to go to a teachers' training college in London, some time in the eighties: and there he found Education, a prize, a jewel, not a modern convenience laid on like hot and cold water ... (*Margin Released*)

Jonathan Priestley was a socialist. He wasn't a socialist of the doctrinaire kind; his socialism was of the old-fashioned English kind, shaped more by Methodism than by Marxism. He wanted to relieve suffering, he wanted to bring light out of darkness, he wanted to leave the world a better place than he found it. The spirit which moved him was warm and generous and compassionate, and the reforms which he helped to bring about – school dinners are one notable example – of the solid and practical kind which did indeed make the world a better place. He was a father to look up to, a father for a son to model himself upon; but to model oneself upon someone is far from being the same thing as to copy:

Though largely tolerant and humorous, there was a curious puritanical streak in him. One of our differences was that from childhood I was fascinated by any form of professional entertainment, whereas he was suspicious of it, considering it at best a waste of time, and possibly a danger to sound character building ... He was also a fanatical Sabbatarian ... (*Margin Released*)

He was, in short, like most of us, a bundle of contradictions, but he was essentially a good and loveable man. Priestley was happy at home, and his home was, most important of all, a bookish one.

His mother died soon after he was born. 'I do not remember my mother at all,' he told me. 'But I was told she was lively and witty and was once turned out of a theatre for laughing in the wrong place – bless her heart! She was probably a mill girl.' Her family was in a different stratum of the Bradford working class from his father's. His

9

father's family belonged to the superior working class, the respectable working class, she came 'from the clogs and shawls and back o't mill, a free and easy, rather raffish kind of working class life, where in the grim little back-to-back houses they shouted and screamed, laughed and cried, and sent out a jug for more beer ...'.

There is a temptation to generalize sweepingly here, to have his mother represent emotional vitality and his father intellectual stamina, the one symbolizing the great steed and the other the rider. Apart from any other consideration his father too was lively and witty, in no sense the cool intellectual. The image does, however, have some sort of correspondence with the facts. His father and mother married because each recognized in the other a special awareness and eagerness, something above the ordinary.

Priestley's early childhood, because of the death of his mother, was not a happy one: 'Something was missing that should have been there.' His time in the infant class at Whetley Lane Primary School was, as he remembered nearly eighty years later, in *Instead of The Trees*, a miserable one:

The woman I remember there obviously disliked me ... I remember my own terror and despair, at an age when you don't realize that time may soon change everything, when you feel small, helpless and apparently doomed, arriving day after day with fear curdling your inside ...

But time – and his father's remarriage – did indeed change everything. Once out of the infant's class, he was 'out of those dark areas into some sunlight, beginning to enjoy my passion for books and games, doing well at school in all things ...'. Here at the very beginning we are shown his extraordinary inner strength. For it is precisely in the years before five that the foundations of character are laid, that the psyche is shaped irreversibly. The Priestley family was not a nuclear family; there would have been women to look after the child and in particular his grandmother. And he had a loving and deeply responsible father. Nevertheless, no blow could have been more severe. A lesser man could well have been emotionally crippled, one way or another. Perhaps there is one scar: Priestley has never written about young children from the inside, so to speak.

His step-mother 'defied tradition by being always kind, gentle, loving'. He was happy at home and won a scholarship to Belle Vue Grammar School, where his father had once taught. He continued to be happy at home even after he had announced his decision to leave school. At the age of seventeen he went to work as a junior clerk with a wool firm, Helm and Company, Swan Arcade, Bradford. It would have been understandable for his father to have fiercely objected to his decision to leave school. It would not only have been natural for him to have wished his son to have the supreme advantage of a university education, perhaps even follow in his footsteps, but he also might well have felt, knowing his son's imaginative and bookish temperament, that he would be far happier at a university. With the best intentions in the world, he could have made his son's life a misery or even a disaster, by attempting to assert his will over him by treating him as an extension of himself, by having him lead the life he would have chosen for himself. But he loved him properly – which is to say unselfishly – and regarded him as an individual and separate person, capable of making his own choices.

Priestley's decision was in fact not on the face of it a sensible one. For him to go into the wool trade was his father's choice and he had no enthusiasm for it. What he was clear about was that he was tired of school. He had always done well there, but now he didn't want any more of it. He wasn't in the least attracted by Oxbridge – 'Nothing beckoned there. I didn't see myself in courts or quads, under dreaming spires; and nine years and a long war later, when finally I did arrive in Cambridge I still didn't see myself there, never felt at home.'

The decision was in fact an instinctive one. At the age of sixteen it could hardly have been otherwise. It was a decision too important to be decided by reason. For at the age of sixteen the mould which shapes the rest of one's life is being set. It can't be changed in adult-hood except by an almost inhuman act of will. The Oxbridge mould would have been the wrong one. 'I wanted to write ... and I believed that the world outside classroom and labs would help me to become a writer ...'

For Oxbridge would have cut him off from the real world. It was then – it still is even now – the world of the scholar and the gentleman, of the enclosed garden, that Oxbridge represents. It would have been too small and too airless for Priestley, and its danger for him would have been that it would have recognized his talents and chained him there for the rest of his life.

He didn't consider what would have seemed to most sixteen-year-olds in his position an attractive alternative:

> I wanted to write but I had just enough sense to know that I must spend at least the next few years trying my hand at it. I also knew – and this was clever of me at sixteen – that work on a newspaper was no good to me, otherwise I would have rejected the wool trade and bluffed or wheedled myself into one of our three local dailies.

And here again there would have been a danger of his talents being recognized, of offers being made which he couldn't refuse, of his true vocation being gradually diverted into the wrong channels, and even of being cut off from reality. For the relationship of the journalist to his material is totally different from that of the creative writer. And, over and above all that, to be an employee, not to have been his own man, would have been death to him. It was not clever of him to reject the idea of work for a paper, any more than it was clever of him to reject the idea of Oxbridge. It was the feminine side of his nature taking over. This has nothing to do with sex: I speak of the instinctive side of his nature, the side of his nature which was directed from the deepest levels.

The job at Helm and Company was ill-paid and dull, the working day from nine to six (and sometimes seven) Monday to Friday, and nine to half past one on a Saturday. Priestley hated the job. He admitted, some fifty years later in *Margin Released*, that he was very bad at it:

> Why I wasn't sacked after the first few months, I couldn't imagine then. It must have been obvious that I did not take the business seriously. I was lazy and careless; I wore what were by Bradford trade standards outlandish clothes; the time I took on any errand outside the office was monstrous, a scandal. True, I was paid very little, but even on that low rate I was a bad bargain ...

But he did not seriously worry about this. The part of his life which really mattered was being led outside the office. There was first and foremost his writing in the front attic at home:

A small gas-fire had been installed there ... On the colour-washed walls I pinned reproductions of pictures I liked. I cut and trimmed some orange boxes, which really looked like bookcases, at least in artificial light. Most of the books in them I had been able to buy only by spending tuppence instead of the eightpence I was allowed for lunch ... Between the bed and the gas-fire, a fierce little thing which could not begin to warm the room without grilling your shins, there was just enough space for two smallish old armchairs, so that when I was not scribbling and scribbling away, I could entertain a friend ... I was immensely proud of this room of mine ... Once I had climbed those stairs and closed the door behind me, I was no longer a junior wool clerk. I was a writer-poet, story-teller, humorist, commentator and social philosopher, at least in my own estimation ...

And from 1913 he began to be published, his first acceptance being an imaginary interview, 'Secrets of the Ragtime King' in *London Opinion*, for which he was paid a guinea, which at that time bought twenty new hardback books, nearly four pounds of good tobacco, or a week's holiday. He also from January to October of that year wrote a column – unpaid – for a Bradford Labour weekly, the *Bradford Pioneer*. He wasn't a member of the Labour Party and didn't take any active part in politics, and has never done so to this day. The column was made up of notices about books and concerts and plays. He was learning the craft of writing in the only possibly way, which was to practise it at every opportunity. He was also acquiring the experience of writing to length and to a deadline, he was preparing himself to be a professional. From the first he never seems to have been the sort of writer who produces draft after draft, an obsessive tinkerer unwilling to let his work go, afraid to face editorial judgement. He has always been an easy writer who has made easy reading.

Looking at those years from 1911 to 1914 one cannot see how he could have crammed in more. For his limited spare time – most evenings he could not have reached home before seven and most Saturday afternoons before two – was not entirely taken up with writing. There was the theatre, there were concerts, there were explorations of the countryside, there were friends and even a café life at Lyon's in Market Street, and there were girls. And what girls meant to him at that age in that era was enchantment: there would have been no question of actual sexual intercourse and kisses would have been the summit of each affair, to be dreamed about long after. Sex, for the majority of young men, came only with marriage. There was, of course, a permissive society in Bradford – there was more than one brothel and they all did a roaring trade, and more than one pillar of society kept a young mistress on the side – but it comprised a tiny minority and it kept very quiet about it. But for young men like Priestley sex was in every sense of the word a pure enchantment.

Priestley does not feel that he has missed anything. On the contrary, he feels that he has gained. He has memories of sex with no bitterness and no pain, remembering, for instance, the open-air concerts in Lister Park where young people paraded on a summer's evening, picking each other up, in an entirely spontaneous and wholly innocent mating ritual:

The place and the hour were propitious for mating: a summer evening, trees and grass between, youth and the dark narrow streets; the hills above the tree-tops fading into dusk; all the people, thousands and thousands of them, sitting, standing, or in the slow river of faces on the promenade; the lighted bandstand in the haze below, a glitter of instruments, the scarlet flash of a uniform, coming through the blue air, and music coming too, not recognisable, not attended to, a long way off, but music. A good time, a good place, for the beginning of love.

Bradford was his city, and it held all that he needed. He did not dream of London, but of a cottage on the moors and a pound a week. He did not dream of rising out of his class, because he did not think of class. 'When, about thirty years ago, Bernard Shaw came back from Russia, he told me it was a wonderful relief to be in a country that had no ladies and gentlemen. I said that I had spent the first twenty years of my life without meeting any of these ladies and gentlemen.' It wasn't that Bradford didn't have a social hierarchy: but it wasn't based upon what one's father did and where one went to school. It was based upon what one personally had accomplished. And there was no forelock-tugging, no bowing and scraping. 'Wool men who gambled and won generally left Bradford before they acquired a title and began entertaining the County. If they had come back, a lot of men wearing cloth caps and mufflers would still have called them Sam and Joe.' And Bradford provided Priestley with all that he needed to nourish him as a writer. He didn't need to go to London. Bradford had theatres, a concert hall, a thriving cultural life. And it wasn't a city which died in the evening, it wasn't a city in which anyone needed to be lonely. Everyone knew everyone in Bradford – and indeed were probably related to each other. And, though not a beautiful city, it had its own identity, it was a real place, it could be loved. Within easy reach was the most beautiful country in the world, the Yorkshire Dales. If Priestley turned to the right at the end of Saltburn Terrace, within ten minutes' walk he would see the road sweep down breathtakingly into Cottingley, the whole valley before him. From Cottingley it was only a short journey to Bingley, from Bingley only a short journey to the pub Dick Hudson's (the name of a former owner) and the beginning of the walk to Ilkley Moors, with short springy turf under the feet, the curlews crying, the drystone walls as if growing naturally out of the earth, the air clean and bracing, with a cool breeze even on the hottest day. The moors were not desolate, they were austere, they were not bleak, they were intoxicating with their sense of space, wildness, freedom. One was always aware of their proximity as in a seaport one is always aware of the sea.

Priestley made no plans for the future but used his time to the utmost. The era encouraged him. Bradford was progressive and alive, a reforming city, a pioneering city. It was not only the city in which every bright boy or girl had a chance of a grammar school education, it was also the city in which Margaret Macmillan set up her first school for handicapped children. It was the cradle of the Independent Labour Party, it was a powerhouse of social change. It was also tough and dour. It wouldn't tell the young, so to speak, how splendid their aspirations were: it would tell them to put up or shut up, whatever they did it would challenge them to go one better. It was Priestley's home town and those years from 1911 to 1914 irrevocably set their stamp on him. He is an international, not a regional writer, a citizen of the world. But no one thinks of him without thinking of Bradford. 'Part of me is still in Bradford, can never leave it, though when I return there now, I wander about half-lost, a melancholy stranger.'

In early September 1914 he joined the 10th Duke of Wellington's. He did not join up for patriotic reasons, he did not join up because all his friends were joining. He did not know at the time why he was going to war. He believes now that once again it was a matter of obeying his instincts. 'I went at a signal from the unknown ... There came, out of the unclouded blue of that summer, a challenge that was almost like a conscription of the spirit, little to do really with King and Country and flag-waving and hip-hip-hurrah, a challenge to our untested manhood.'

He speaks about the 1914 War with pain and grief, to this day. During the war – and particularly when he was commissioned – he first encountered the English class system. The army he joined was commanded by English gentlemen – gentlemen first, officers a long way after – who combined impenetrable stupidity with impenetrable complacency. Nothing in his experience had prepared him for what he was to undergo. Nothing like it had happened in the world's history. The British army had made its mistakes in the past but these mistakes had been as often as not the consequence of individual ineptitude or of unforeseen mischance. The Charge of the Light Brigade had been a blunder: an order had been misinterpreted. It had not been intended to have cavalry charge the guns; even Raglan knew his business better than that. In the 1914 War it was as if the Charge of the Light Brigade had been ordered by the High Command a thousand times a day. There were only bouts of slaughter, not battles, in the 1914 War, as Winston Churchill pointed out in *The World Crisis 1911–1919*. 'Battles,' he said,

are won by slaughter and manœuvre. The greater the general, the more he contributes in manœuvre, the less he demands in slaughter. The theory which has elevated the '*bataille d'usure*' or 'battle of wearing down' into a foremost position is contradicted by history and would be repulsed by the greatest generals in the past ... There is required for the composition of a great commander not only massive common sense and reasoning power, not only imagination, but also an element of legerdemain, an original and sinister touch, which leaves the enemy puzzled as well as beaten. It is because military leaders are credited with gifts of this order which

16

enable them to ensure victory and save slaughter that their profession is held in such high honour. For if their art were nothing more than a dreary process of exchanging lives, and counting heads in the end, they would rank much lower, in the scale of human esteem.

Priestley went out to France with the Duke of Wellington's in the summer of 1915 and was for some time in the region of Neuve Chapelle. The regiment then moved south and took over Vimy Ridge and Souchez from the French. In June 1916 Priestley was buried alive, injured and partly deafened by a big trench mortar. He was rushed back to England, was in hospital for some weeks, then spent a long time in convalescent camps. He then took a commission in the Devon Regiment. He went out to the front again in the summer of 1918, but was partly gassed during an attack in the early autumn. That was his last glimpse of action in the 1914 War and he was discharged from hospital unfit for active service. Shortly after his discharge from hospital the Armistice was declared, and he left the army finally in the early spring of 1919. He had gone into the war, as he says in *Margin Released*, 'free of any class feeling'. He left the army 'with a chip on my shoulder; a big heavy chip, probably some friend's thigh-bone'.

We now have to consider a mystery. Why did Priestley not write a major novel on the theme of the 1914 War? His own answer is that, first of all, when he left the army he wanted 'to get on with my life, to look forward and not back'. He also found that he was 'deeply divided between the tragedy and the comedy of it'. He could not reconcile these two elements. This is fair enough; but personally I consider that there are even stronger reasons. I think that the 1914 War, if used as material even ten years after, would have warped him creatively. It would have kept the poison in the bloodstream, it would have damaged him as a human being and as a writer. I consider that once again he obeyed his instincts and stored the experience away, to be used eventually at one remove, as it was in *An Inspector Calls*. It is in fact always there, and is one of the themes underlying his social philosophy. There are more ways of using an experience than writing directly about it.

There is another explanation. The period of primal experience for a creative writer ends at some time in the early twenties. When the writer is no longer in the process of becoming a writer but actually is one, then experience becomes something different. It isn't that it is no longer absorbed or that it never was observed: it's that the emphasis is upon observation rather than upon absorption. A writer is like other men in that he has the same experiences and, broadly speaking, the same emotional reactions to them. But in himself he isn't in the least like other men. He is almost of a different species. With Priestley the process of becoming a writer, the change, one might almost say, from human being to writer, was made even more radical by his experiences as a front-line soldier. The human being, John Boynton Priestley, was killed during the 1914 War. He was born again as a writer. He wasn't a man who wrote: he was – and is – all writer, as no one else before or since. Whenever he used memories from the period of primal experience, he wouldn't use his own memories but the memories of a dead man whom he'd known as well as himself. This of course is a wholly fantastic and wildly inaccurate way of putting it, but it's as near to the actual truth as I can get.

2

The Sorcerer Begins His Journey

Priestley took his degree in modern history and political science at Trinity Hall, Cambridge, in 1921. In 1919 he had married Pat Tempest, the daughter of a neighbour, whom he had got to know by playing duets for violin and piano. His ex-army grant had never been adequate and he had had to supplement it by writing, coaching, and lecturing. He left Cambridge in 1922 to freelance in London with fifty pounds capital and almost certain that his wife was pregnant. He had been offered a job as a Cambridge Extension lecturer in North Devon, but had turned it down.

Once again he was following his instincts, rejecting the easy and obvious way. The rejection was 'a decision received with bitter incredulity at home in Bradford'. It was not, however, quite as reckless as it would seem. He already had a foothold in literary journalism, a degree and some experience in lecturing, and had had his first book, *Brief Diversions*, a collection of essays, published in 1922. It had had good notices but the sales had been slow. Nevertheless, as a freelance writer with a book behind him, he was then in a position of strength. As he pointed out in *Margin Released*, 'it was easier for a young writer in the early Twenties to earn a living than it is today'. He said this in 1962; the position for the freelance writer has become even worse since then. Priestley estimated in 1964 that in the early Twenties there was ten times as much space for the freelance writer; in 1978 that figure can be doubled, the market having shrunk still further, and there is in addition the National Union of Journalists' closed shop. The freelance writer can't publish enough to earn a living unless he's an NUJ member; but he won't be admitted to membership unless he's earning a substantial amount – enough for a living – through journalism. And even if he is one of the few who writes a successful novel or TV series, tax is so savage that, unless his way of living is positively ascetic, he never has the chance to accumulate a reserve. More and more the young writer, particularly if he is married, is forced into being an employee.

This is what Priestley never was. He earned his living in the only way a writer should earn his living, by selling his work in the open market. Not only was there more space then for reviews, articles, and short stories in periodicals like the *London Mercury*, the *Bookman*, and the *Saturday Review*, but newspapers devoted far more space to outside contributions in general and reviews in particular. (It's worth noting that there was then a wide market for the short story and that now the market is virtually non-existent.) He was also paid six pounds a week as reader to the Bodley Head. Six pounds a week was then a living wage. Among the books which he discovered was C. S. Forester's *The General*, possibly the best novel about the 1914 War, and unfortunately overshadowed to this day by the Hornblower series.

By 1925 he had published five books. Three of them were collections of essays, two of them works of criticism. He was now a professional. And he was, in his own words, 'giving my bookish half a freer run'. He still was not consciously and coolly planning his career, but writing, as always, only what he wanted to write.

He was also meeting other authors. There was in the Twenties still a literary London, chiefly because authors could then afford to live in London. He wasn't in the least interested in playing literary politics but he enjoyed the company of Shaw, Wells, Arnold Bennett, Robert Lynd, Hilaire Belloc and Sir James Barrie among others. He felt that writers should meet, that they had much to give each other, that at least they could help each other to take the curse off their occupational disease of loneliness, get rid of the feeling of their difficulties being unique, learn that others are plagued by them too:

It is all too easy for a young writer, as he tails on and on alone, deep in his own world, to begin to feel that what he is doing is shadowy, unreal, a laborious nonsense. If he meets other writers then he finds himself with men and women, now smiling, who have also known and have escaped from that treacherous dream.

The war was over and his life was full and happy. For happiness is the great bonus of doing the work one was born to do. Then in 1924 his father died of cancer. And in 1925, after a long illness, his wife died of cancer, leaving him with two small daughters, Barbara and Sylvia. He had worked through the long agony of his wife's illness. He had had no alternative: the expense of that illness in the era before the Welfare State would have been heavy. As an employee he might have been given time off; but the self-employed are paid only for work delivered. The cost of freedom can be high. But the real writer pays it. A real writer, a professional, writes no matter what he feels like. He doesn't wait for inspiration. Whoever waits for inspiration isn't a writer.

It was at this time that Priestley began his book on George Meredith. He began it when he was living at Chinnor Hill on the far edge of the Chilterns, visiting his wife regularly at Guy's Hospital. He returned home one afternoon 'deep in despair'. Simply to occupy his mind, he looked at the rough list of characters for the Meredith book. 'I chose one of the chapters, not the first, and, slowly, painfully, set to work on it. In an hour I was writing freely and well. It is in fact one of the best chapters of the book. And I wrote myself out of my misery, followed a trail of thought and words into daylight.'

I have had no such tragedy in my life, but I have had my bad moments, and I here gratefully acknowledge how much this passage has helped me. I am not only in debt to him for the pleasure his work has given me. Priestley lived through his tragedy, kept on writing, kept on writing well, kept on marching towards the sound of the guns. There were no less than nine more books in the next three years. He married Jane, the former wife of D. B. Wyndham Lewis the satirist, in 1926 and began to build a new life. By Jane he had a son Tom and two daughters, Mary and Rachel. His stepdaughter, Angela Wyndham Lewis, from the first became one of the family. 'I used always to say', his friend Norman Collins told me, that the two best smiles in England were the Queen Mother's and Jane Priestley's. She was pretty, dark-haired, Welsh. She'd read for Modern Languages and was a fluent French speaker. She was very interested in bird-watching and I in fact was associated in publishing her *Book of Birds* for Gollancz. It was a very good introduction to the subject with illustrations by Tunnicliffe. Jane was a natural hostess. I remember that at their Isle of Wight home there were five children, a nanny, butler, and other servants, and that every weekend they seemed to have house guests. Fourteen for dinner was commonplace. Everyone who wanted to ride had horses – Jane not only ran this very large establishment like clockwork but organized rides for all the guests too. She was a marvellous organizer and she had superb good taste in planning their homes; every detail – furniture, carpets, decorations and so on – were exactly right.

The nine books comprised three collections of essays – *Talking, Open House, Apes and Angels* – four works of criticism – *George Meredith, Peacock, The English Novel, English Humour* – and two novels, *Adam in Moonshine* and *Benighted*. All can be read with pleasure to this day. The Meredith book in particular is more than 'on the edge of criticism', it is a valuable contribution to the understanding of an unjustly neglected writer. It isn't criticism in the sense that it is a work of academic analysis. It is an interpretation of Meredith, it is a clear exposition of why we should read him. The essays, as with all his essays, have the quality of good conversation, they are sane and civilized and humane, more relaxed than Addison but in the same tradition.

What is fascinating about his early work is that in the first place he began his career with his prose already a perfect instrument. There is no difference between the quality of the prose in his first book and his hundredth book. One couldn't, presuming for the sake of argument that one hadn't any knowledge of him and all evidence of the year of writing had been removed, date Priestley's work by his prose, as one could, for example, with Scott Fitzgerald. It is almost as if he had somehow perfected his style before he began to write. His concern is with his subject, not his style. He doesn't, as it were, experiment with pencils until he finds the right one. He chose the right pencil at the beginning and it always keeps sharp.

Secondly – as Alan Sillitoe has remarked about Arnold Bennett

– his style for non-fiction is the same as for fiction. It's a generalization which no doubt can easily be disproved, but virtually all writers of my generation have two styles. Our prose for fiction is different from our prose for non-fiction. We change gear when, for instance, we write a review. We are specialists. And our prose is none the better for it. Our prose for fiction is too literary, our prose for non-fiction too conversational. We are either too formal or too unbuttoned: there is a middle way which we haven't found, and because we haven't found it we don't reach far enough, we don't give all that we have to give. It's as if we either goosestepped or shuffled, our hands in our pockets. Priestley's prose is in the moorland walker's style, easy and natural, covering the distance unwearingly. For the writers he modelled himself upon in his youth were not alienated from the people, there was no gap between serious writing on the one hand and entertainment on the other, it was not considered that whatever was popular automatically must be dismissed as being totally without literary merit.

The most astounding year of all was 1927 when he published no fewer than five books, including his first two novels, total wordage at the lowest count of a quarter of a million. One full-length novel would be thought of as being a good year's work by the majority of writers. If one has any complaint against Priestley at all, it is that his enormous productivity makes the rest of us feel lazy and inadequate, mere dilettantes. *Benighted*, most astoundingly of all, was written late at night after a full day's work on another book. There is no sign of strain in any of the five books, no trace of scamping.

Adam in Moonshine, his first novel, was moderately successful in Britain and 'an instant and devastating failure' in America. It's essentially a 'light fantastic farcical tale', the story of a young man, Adam Stewart, who is mistaken for the true heir to the English throne by a secret society, the Companions of the Rose. There are beautiful girls, including a Russian temptress with whom Adam almost goes to bed, a formidable Inspector and his not very bright Sergeant, a beautiful mansion in the Yorkshire Dales, good food and good wine and escapes and chases with no one hurt in the end. The high spirits are consistently sustained and the narrative all hangs together. Adam is rather more than a lay figure: he is genuinely a young man, eager for adventure and romance, with all his life before him. Taken for what it is, a light confection, a meringue, a soufflé, it still can be enjoyed. Already evident is Priestley's great merit as a novelist, which is fullness of treatment. All the characters are described and their background is three-dimensional.

Priestley describes it and its successor *Benighted* as 'experiments which failed'. What he was trying to do – based upon his wide reading and criticism of contemporary fiction – was to reconcile two very different approaches. He wanted to tell a straightforward story whilst looking inside his characters. If he didn't present the thoughts and moods of his characters then they would have no depth, they'd be merely puppets. It seemed to him that contemporary novels, if they told a story, didn't look inside the characters and, if they looked inside the characters, didn't tell a story, and so were psychological studies rather than novels. (Possibly he had Virginia Woolf in mind.) Before he wrote his first novel, he had to find a way out of this dilemma which faced him 'like a lion in the path'.

Benighted – published in the USA as *The Old Dark House* – is much more sombre than *Adam in Moonshine*. Philip and Margaret Waverton and Roger Penderel are forced into taking shelter in the house of Horace Femm and his sister one dark and stormy night somewhere in Wales. The roads are flooded; there is nowhere else to go. They are joined by another pair of benighted travellers, Sir William Porterhouse and his young mistress Gladys Du Cane. The Femms, a half-crazed, grotesque old couple, are strangely reluctant to give them shelter. The mysteries pile up; there is another Femm upstairs, Sir Roderick. Sir Roderick is bedridden, along with his memories, none of which are happy. The house has never been a happy house. And what is the real function of Morgan, the huge and half-witted servant? Who else is upstairs besides Sir Roderick? This time Priestley doesn't end with no one harmed; there are two violent deaths. But there is a happy ending of sorts. Philip and Margaret have been brought closer together and Sir William has been revealed as a decent and compassionate human being. What does stick in the mind is that the deaths are absolutely convincing, that here for the first and last time he made direct use of his wartime experience. Penderel is still shell-shocked, shell-shocked in the sense that he almost welcomes violent death, that he fights without hatred. He doesn't enjoy killing: but he is perhaps impatient that his rendezvous with death has been delayed so long.

Priestley's next novel, *Farthing Hall*, was written in collaboration with Hugh Walpole and published in 1929. The collaboration was suggested by Walpole, who knew that his name would ensure a large advance. With his share of the advance Priestley was able to buy the time to write the long novel which he had had in mind for some time. Long novels, incidentally, were not then looked upon favourably by publishers. He had to give it his undivided attention, he had to be free of all other commitments. *Farthing Hall*, a straightforward romance in letter form, was duly finished. He now had the time. And a new phase in his life was beginning.

3

The Crowded Page

The enormous success of *The Good Companions*, published in 1929, marked the emergence of J. B. Priestley as a name and as a myth. The myth, nearly fifty years later, is still with us. It is the myth of the hard-headed and coarse-grained Yorkshireman who knew exactly what the public liked and who gave them it, his only motive being the desire to make a great deal of money. What follows from this is a refusal by a part at least of the critical establishment ever again to take him seriously as a creative writer, much less a social thinker.

Norman Collins, who first met him in 1928 at the old *Daily News* (later the liberal *News Chronicle*, a paper with which Priestley had a long connection), remembers a significant incident soon after the publication of *The Good Companions*. Robert Lynd, the literary editor of the *News Chronicle*, was the central figure of a

genuine literary salon. Of course the part of Hampstead where he lived was a very literary part of London. Near Lynd were writers like Viola Garvin, Victor Gollancz, Charles Morgan – at the Lynds', in fact, one would meet just about every writer who was worth reading. Robert Lynd was in the best sense of the word the sweetest of men, almost saint-like – we became friends, and it was very pleasant for a young man without money to go to his house and meet these writers. Lynd once gave a party at the Hampstead Conservatory. There was an adoring group round Arnold Bennett, drinking in every word. Then Priestley came in. They absolutely melted away from Bennett – if I hadn't seen it, I wouldn't have believed it – and all clustered round Priestley. Mind you – and this is important – I don't think that Jack gave a damn.

Once the myth had emerged, it had a life of its own, it couldn't be restrained by facts. The facts were that *The Good Companions* was Priestley's seventeenth book and fourth novel and that he had built up a solid reputation and, though far from being rich, was very far from being poor. The myth stated firmly that *The Good Companions* was not only Priestley's first novel but his first book and had catapulted him from indigent obscurity overnight. As Norman Collins said:

His earliest essays and his literary criticism were outstandingly good. Then the colossal success of *The Good Companions* made everyone forget these achievements. It was the same with his plays and perhaps most of all with *Time and the Conways*. They blotted out the achievement of his novels. And yet again the success of the wartime Postscripts blotted out everything else. That's the story of his life.

There are other elements of the myth which are worth noting. There is the notion that one best-selling novel makes the author's fortune once and for all. No matter what ventures may go disastrously wrong, he isn't ever supposed to be in need of money again. But, of course, since he is now not a serious writer but a best-seller, then everything which he writes will be a best-seller. (It was not a myth which was current before the 1914 War. Reviewers then took it for granted that sales had no relevance to a book's literary merit one way or another.)

The truth, of course, is completely different. J. B. Priestley didn't know what the public wanted when he wrote *The Good Companions*. Nobody knows what the public wants. No publisher knows what the public wants. In J. B. Priestley's own words, the public itself doesn't know what it wants until it gets it. And absolutely the only motive compelling enough to make one write any novel, much less as long a novel as *The Good Companions*, is the sheer joy of creation. Being human, and needing money as much as anyone else, the novelist indeed hopes for huge sales. But there isn't room in his head for anything else but the novel itself once he begins it. There is no room for anything else but joy – the most arduous joy in the world, but the most deeply satisfying.

When Orson Welles saw his first film set he's reported to have exclaimed: 'This is the best train set a boy ever had.' There is much of this sense of immense and entrancing technical resources evident in *The Good Companions*. This indeed is what has kept it fresh: all throughout Priestley is rejoicing in his powers. And, once and for all, he has left the subjective novel behind him. He is looking outside himself rather than inwards, and he is looking at society as much as at individual characters.

It is indeed in one sense an escapist novel. All the leading characters escape from what are in one way and another confining or even actively miserable and hopeless lives into happy endings. Like H. G. Wells's Mr Polly, they each discover that if you don't like your life you can change it. It is a genuine picaresque novel, a story of adventures on the open road. This is part of its appeal: one doesn't know what will happen next. To quote H. G. Wells again, it may even be worse than anything that one has experienced before but at least it will be different – perhaps even dangerous and disastrous but never boring.

Here it is important to make a point which is not purely literary: communicated in *The Good Companions* is the unconquerability of the human spirit. The characters are not running away *from*; they are running towards. They haven't given up the battle; they've opened up a new front. And a picture comes through of the author. He is a man who, like Hemingway's Colonel Cantwell, never feels sad in the morning. Even if nothing went right yesterday, he hopes that something wonderful will happen today. He isn't a fool and expects no glittering handouts. He will endure all that he has to endure, but not passively: he is sustained always by that moment of joy in the morning. This is J. B. Priestley's literary *persona*; in *The Good Companions* he establishes it for the first time. This *persona* cannot be established by any conscious effort and never by being explicitly autobiographical. It is not described. It is *there*, and so is one's audience.

The actual story of *The Good Companions* is very simple. The period is approximately the time at which it was written. Miss Elizabeth Trant, a colonel's daughter in her thirties and on the verge of resigning herself to spinsterhood, finds herself on her father's death the inheritor of £1,530, a small cottage, and an income, after letting the family home, of £300 a year. These figures are all specified; the novel wouldn't get off the ground if they weren't. (It must, of course, be borne in mind that to arrive at a present-day comparison all these figures must be multiplied by at least fifteen.) Miss Trant, now independent, is overcome by the need for change. 'She seemed to have had a suddenly terrible glimpse of life as it really was, and was ready to weep at the thought of its strange dusty littleness.'

She buys a little two-seater car from her nephew for £150, and sets off on impulse on what is ostensibly a tour of the cathedrals of England but is actually a tour to wherever the impulse takes her. She meets by chance – this is an understatement – Jess Oakroyd, a joiner from Bruddersford who has left his home and a nagging wife, Inigo Jollifant, a schoolmaster who has also left his job, Morton Mitcham, an old-fashioned barn-stormer who is, as they say, resting, and the members of a touring concert party, The Dinky Doos, who have been stranded by their manager. She takes over the management of the Dinky Doos, changes the name to the Good Companions, and we go on from there.

It is almost the archetypally well-made novel. It's divided into three parts of roughly equal length, the third being the shortest. In Book One we are introduced to the leading characters and see them come together. In Book Two we see them as the Good Companions, a new entity. And it all happens, we're in the thick of it. And in Book Three it's all wound up with no loose ends and everyone's dreams come true. There is even an Epilogue, a brief and graceful summary, a farewell to the audience. In short, the structure of the novel is that of the traditional well-made play. It isn't used because the theme is the adventures of a theatrical troupe. It is used because it solves a problem.

That is how to combine complexity and richness with simplicity. At any moment in a narrative of well over a quarter of a million words the reader must know where he is. If he doesn't, if he's mystified but not agreeably mystified, then he'll be no longer carried along by the story, he won't be interested in what happens next. The true novelist never explains: as soon as explanations begin, the narrative grinds to a halt. He *shows*.

At the beginning of the book none of the three main characters knows of one another's existence, much less of the Dinky Doos. And for each one of them the notion of involvement with a travelling concert party isn't within the realms of possibility. That's another element in the story. When Jess Oakroyd, having lost his job, tears up his insurance card and says he's going south, when Miss Trant sets off to Ely in her little blue two-seater, when Inigo walks briskly away from the dreary private school on a dark cold night, they have their dreams but their dreams have no precise shape.

The point of view in Book One is over the shoulders of each of the main characters. What must be stressed is that we do exactly that: we look over their shoulders, we don't look deep into their minds. The first person we look at is not Miss Trant, who'd be the obvious choice, since without her there can't be the Good Companions. The obvious choice is the amateur's choice and means that we're signalling our punches, telling the reader what will happen before it happens. We don't, to be accurate, look at any person in the beginning:

There, far below, is the knobbly backbone of England, the Pennine Range. At first, the whole dark length of it, from the Peak to Cross Fell, is visible. Then the Derbyshire hills and the Cumberland fells disappear, for you are descending, somewhere about the middle of the range ... where the high moorland thrusts itself between the woollen mills of Yorkshire and the cotton mills of Lancashire ...

We descend further, circling down to the long smudge of smoke, beneath which the towns of the West Riding lie buried ... Descending again, we at last see the shape of the towns but only as a blacker edge to the high moorland, so many fantastic outcroppings of its rock ...

And then we are in Bruddersford (which basically of course is Bradford), we see its Town Hall, its mills, its public buildings, we move from the centre to Manchester Road to join the crowd leaving the football grounds and to meet Jess Oakroyd:

Somewhere in the middle of this tide of cloth caps is one that is different from its neighbours. It is neither grey nor green but a rather dirty brown. Then, unlike most of the others, it is not too large for its wearer but, if anything, a shade too small, though it is true he has pushed it back from his forehead as if he were too hot – as indeed he is. The cap and the head

it has almost ceased to decorate are both the property of a citizen of Bruddersford, an old and enthusiastic supporter of the United Football Club,
whose name is Josiah Oakroyd ... known as 'Jess'. He is a working man
between forty-five and fifty years of age, a trifle under medium height but
stockily built. Neither ugly nor handsome, with a blunt nose, a moustache
that may have been once brisk and fair but is now ragged and mousey, and
blue eyes that regard the world pleasantly enough but with just a trace of
either wonder or resentment or both ...

The enormous technical accomplishment of this beginning can
only be properly valued if we examine the alternatives. The first is
a straightforward description of the Pennine Range, the country
round Bruddersford, and Bruddersford itself moving into the football crowd and Jess Oakroyd. But take away the image of the great
bird circling – the *implicit* image of great height and the intensifying
view – and what we would have would be something essentially
static. Because of the sense of swooping down as a hawk swoops
down on its prey the story begins with the first words.

Miss out the description or merely sketch it in, and we merely
sketch in Jess Oakroyd. He is himself wherever he is physically situ-
ated. But he is the sort of person he is because he is so typically a
native of Bruddersford. In describing Bruddersford and its surround-
ings we are also in part describing him. He is an authentic and solid
character because his background has been made solid and authentic
to us. The alternative of having the description of his background
follow his description as a person is unsatisfactory too, because it
would hold up the action. It would be making Bruddersford into
a sort of stage set to be dropped into position. And this would be
to falsify the novel, for it's the story of a journey in which places
are as real as people, and must have identity just as the characters
have identity.

Jess Oakroyd is not the hero of the novel. It isn't, as I have said,
about any one person but about the travelling concert party. But
it's his character which gives the novel its cutting edge, which assures
us that the characters are playing for keeps. He is the backbone of
the novel, just as the Pennine Chain is the backbone of England. As
long as he is there we can believe everything that happens. The
reasons for him leaving home are prosaic enough: he loses his job

through a demarcation dispute, his wife is a dreary shrew, he has nothing in common with his son, and his wife cannot be prevented from taking in as a lodger his son's friend Albert, a young man who he finds thoroughly detestable. On top of this he finds himself richer by twenty pounds and unjustly suspected of robbery. He announces his intention of leaving home; his son calmly hands him his insurance card:

Mr Oakroyd stood staring at the greenish-blue card in his hand, staring as if he were in a dream. *Man – Age 16 to 65 ... Failure to surrender this card promptly ... If the Insured Person ... The Insured Person ...* All so familiar and yet so strange. He stood staring, baffled, lost in the dark of a world of notices and notifying, of sneering Comrades and stupid autocratic managers, of buzzers that kept your feet from the road, of signs that could never be hoisted, of daughters that grew up, laughing and singing, and then vanished over the sea. Then something inside him flared and went shooting through the dark like a rocket, and Mr Oakroyd committed a crime.

'Oh, to hell wi' t'card!' he cried, and tore it across and threw the pieces into the fire ...

It is the irrecoverable act, the rejection of routine, of security, of authority, the symbol of a new life, of irresponsibility and adventure. It is, above all, the act which all wage-earners dream of, then as now: who has not felt that ugly official card to be the brand of servitude?

We move to the Cotswolds and another England:

Here are pleasant green mounds, heights of grass forever stirring to the tune of the southwest wind: clear valleys, each with its gleam of water; grey stone villages, their walls flushing to a delicate pink in the sunlight; parish churches that have rung in and rung out Tudor, Stuart and Hanoverian kings ... here, in the Cotswolds, all is open and pleasant, a Saxon tale of grass and grey stone, wind and clear running water. We have quitted the long war of the north ...

This is the country of the retired and the *rentiers*, the country where money is inherited and money is spent; it is gentle, civilized, and ultimately constricting, a country where imperceptibly youth ebbs away, a prison without bars from which Miss Trant on an impulse releases herself in her little car.

We move to the east and the Fen country:

It is a place plucked from the water. Only here and there remains the old darkly gleaming chaos of marsh and reeds, alders and bulrushes, the sudden whirr and scream of wildfowl. All else is now deep pasturage and immense fields bright with stubble, feeding the windmills and the scattered red-brick farms ... Something desolating certainly remains, a whisper not to be drowned by the creaking of the heaviest harvest-wagon. The little farms seem lonelier than lighthouses. The roads go on and on, one ruled mile after another, but would never appear to arrive anywhere ... The vague sadness of a prairie has fallen upon this plain of dried marshes. Like a rich man who gives but never smiles, this land yields bountifully but is at heart still a wilderness ...

And from Washbury Manor, a private school in the middle of this wilderness, Inigo Jollifant makes his escape. Inigo is

a thin loose-limbed youth, a trifle above medium height. His face does not suggest the successful preparatory school master. It seems rather too fantastic. A long lock of hair falls perpetually across his right eyebrow; his nose itself is long, wandering and whimsical, and his grey eyes are set unusually wide apart and have in them a curious gleam ... There is about him the air of one who is ready to fail gloriously at almost anything ...

Inigo is in fact one of nature's lightweights. His chief ambition is to be a writer; we scarcely need to be told that this ambition will never be fulfilled, for he doesn't take it seriously enough. It's the idea of himself as a writer that he enjoys, not the dreary business of writing. His one real talent, for composing catchy little tunes, he doesn't take seriously at all, and he is so unworldly that he's completely unaware of the commercial value of catchy little tunes. He is unworldly in other ways too. He's highly susceptible to women, but it isn't conceivable that he actually has a sex life. In a way he is more a creature of the footlights, a character in a musical comedy, than any of the other members of the Good Companions.

But this is to forget the different standards of the Twenties when among young men of Inigo's class premarital virginity was the rule rather than the exception. When Inigo leaves Washbury Manor, unable to bear even for another night the abysmal catering and petty tyranny of the Headmaster's virago of a wife, the young School

33

Matron slips out to say goodbye to him and give him some biscuits and chocolate for his journey.

> Inigo was really touched. It came to him in a flash that nobody had done anything like this for him for years. He had been living almost entirely in a world of services for money. 'Daisy Callander,' he cried softly, 'you're a brick. I'm tremendously grateful. I'd forgotten how hungry I should be in an hour or two.'
>
> 'Where are you going?'
>
> He stared at her. 'Do you know, I'd entirely forgotten that. I've no idea where I'm going. I shall just walk and walk. Good-bye – and good luck!' He held out his hand.
>
> She slipped her hand into his instead of shaking it. Then she raised her face a little. 'Good-bye,' she said rather tearfully.
>
> He realised that she wanted him to kiss her. Strangely enough, though he had never liked her more than he did at this moment, he did not want to kiss her. But he did kiss her, gently, then gave her hand a final squeeze ...

He has, in short, seen her not as a female body, an object of desire, but as a kind and decent human being to be taken seriously. The kiss to her has a different value from the kiss to him, and he is sensitive enough to discern it. And, in so doing, to grow up a little.

It would be unfair to potential readers to summarize the way in which Miss Trant meets the Dinky Doos and is inspired to pay the company's debts, rename it as the Good Companions and to make a new life for herself as its manager. It wouldn't have been good enough for her simply to have been in the same place as the Dinky Doos, to overhear their conversation, and on the spur of the moment to offer her help. The events which do bring her and the concert party together must be interesting enough to stand by themselves. The characters who feature in it – though we see none of them again – must be drawn in the round. They are not messengers or commentators to bridge gaps in a few words; they have to be as credible as the other characters, they have to be there in their own right. The story must not determine what the characters do: the story comes out of the characters.

There is no one in *The Good Companions* who is not described, just as there is no place which is not described. If anyone appears, however briefly, if only behind a bar or a counter or delivering a letter, we register their appearance as we would in real life, we notice what they say and how they say it as we would in real life. As Priestley himself says, we don't ever see waiters or shop assistants or postmen with blank faces like oval pieces of plain white cardboard.

For Priestley does not write in the abstract, but in the concrete. He does not *tell* us, he *shows* us. And he leaves nothing out that's necessary for us to know. He doesn't make the mistake of concentrating exclusively upon the Good Companions. For their world, though tough and highly competitive and desperately insecure, is nevertheless a decent world. The talented ones – Jerry Jemingham and Susie Dean – of course are fully aware that they are the stars of the show and that the Good Companions represents only a rung on the ladder. But for all of them there is an ideal of professionalism, a feeling of being part of something larger than themselves. They have values other than money values, they are the creators of a kind of magic; their lives may have been shabby at times, but never sordid.

But there is another world, a mean and ignoble one. It's a world which none of the Good Companions knows very much about. Even their defaulting ex-manager is weak and incompetent rather than wicked; he didn't strand them to enrich himself or out of malice, but simply fled from a situation he couldn't cope with. But in Gatford in the Midlands – a prosperous but hideous town at the centre of the car manufacture country – they come into conflict with Mr Ridvers, who manages the only three cinemas of any importance in the district.

The March wind went shrieking over the Midland Plain. Under a sky as rapid, ragged and tumultuous as a revolution, all the standing water, the gathered thaws and rain of February, filling the dykes and spreading over innumerable fields, was ruffled and whitened, so that the day glittered coldly. There was ice even yet in this wind, but already there were other things too, shreds and tatters of sunlight, sudden spicy gusts, distant trumpetings of green armies on the march ...

We follow the wind to the open window of Mr Ridvers's office:

'For God's sake, Ethel,' he said, 'shut that window. Look at those letters – all over the damned floor. Besides, it's cold.'
From behind her typewriter, Ethel gave him a curious sideways look.

She was a girl in her twenties, with a rather flat Mongolian face, hard staring eyes and a thick daubed mouth. 'It was you who wanted it open,' she remarked. 'Told you it was cold.'

'Well, I want it shut now,' he grunted, without looking up again from the papers in his hand.

'All right, all right,' and she closed the window. There was nothing respectful in her tones, and there was something downright disrespectful in the way she moved. The exaggerated thrust and lift of her shoulders gave the impression that her body was making really impudent remarks about her employer. There was the suggestion that it had the right to make such remarks and that he knew very well that it had.

It transpires that the success of the Good Companions has reduced the takings of Mr Ridvers's cinemas so drastically as to spoil his chances of a worthwhile offer for the cinemas from a syndicate. Worse still, the syndicate may not buy the cinemas at all but build its own. It is made plain that the main reason for the cinemas losing their audiences to the Good Companions is that Mr Ridvers has increased his profit margin by cutting down on maintenance and by renting old films. There is money enough in the district to provide audiences both for the cinemas and the Good Companions. Mr Ridvers isn't really in trouble because of the success of the Good Companions. He's in trouble because he doesn't run his cinemas properly, because he doesn't give the public value for money.

These details emerge incidentally in conversation with Ethel. Ethel, in fact, is very happy to point out how badly his cinemas are doing and how well the Good Companions are doing. This is absolutely in character. Ethel is the mistress of Mr Ridvers, but she detests him. He is a thoroughly detestable man. And the best way of conveying this is not by a flat statement about him – which is merely pinning on a label – but by showing the reactions of those nearest to him. The vital information – which is the key to the climax of the story – is absorbed almost without our knowing it. We remember it not as part of a plot, a piece of a jigsaw puzzle, but as Mr Ridvers, the middle-aged businessman and his young mistress. As he walks towards the hotel where Miss Trant is staying, plagued by the wind and his liver, we could almost feel sorry for him. His attempt at intimidation of Miss Trant fails ignominiously, faced first of all by her cool contempt and then by the formidable presence of Joe Brunt, the company's baritone. He retreats in a towering rage to more drastic measures. Those measures will bring Miss Trant to the verge of ruin – but they will, of course, fail. The destiny of the Good Companions is a happy ending, with each one being given their heart's desire. It is true that Inigo, now a successful song composer, hasn't been able to persuade Susie Dean – now, naturally, a star – to marry him in the end. But perhaps his heart's desire is always to be in love with her and never to run the risk of the disillusionment of marriage.

The book ends as it has begun, with Jess Oakroyd leaving the football match on a Saturday afternoon. But this time he's a widower and not going home but on his way to the railway station and ultimately to Canada to join his daughter. This has been his heart's desire ever since she emigrated to Canada with her husband, and here for the first time is stated one of Priestley's most deeply felt beliefs, to be summarized in Barrie's words: *Daughters are the thing*. We leave Jess, we leave Bruddersford, we are high over the moors, the journey has gone full circle. 'There are the Derbyshire hills and there, away to the north, are the great fells of Cumberland, and now the whole darkening length of it, from the Peak to Cross Fell, is visible, for this is the Pennine Chain, sometimes called the backbone of England.'

I have dealt with *The Good Companions* at some length because it has, since its publication, been grossly undervalued. Primarily because of its enormous success it is now scarcely taken seriously at all as a work of art. It is regarded almost in the same light as the *genre* novel, as the thrillers and the light romances. It is a best-seller, so it can't have anything to say, it can't reflect life as it really is, it is merely a cunningly fabricated and energetically sustained piece of wish-fulfilment for the masses. It is only when one puts aside the matter of its sales, looks at it as if it were published today, that one realizes its extraordinary merits.

The first test it passes is that it doesn't date. It is of its era and Priestley was not detached from that era. What is surprising – for, when he wrote it, the depression was yet to come – is how hard and tough the times were. When Jess Oakroyd loses his job, he is well aware

that it will be almost impossible to find another. He isn't an extrava-
gant man, and has been in employment as a skilled worker since,
presumably, the age of fourteen, if not half-time at school and half-
time at work since eleven, but he has nothing in reserve. When he
sells up his home before his departure to Canada he realizes for the
first time how little he really possesses:

'"By gow! – we live an' learn. I thought once upon a time I'd
gotten a good home together," cried Mr Oakroyd with some bitterness, "but seemingly it's not worth selling up nar."'

And even Miss Trant, who backs the Good Companions, is on
the same razor-edge. If she loses her capital, it will make the difference between comfort and a state not far removed from genteel
poverty. A spinster in her thirties with no training will have no
chance at all of any sort of job. And the Good Companions live in
the world of show business, then as now desperately insecure. Inigo
Jollifant, it's true, doesn't care about the future, being unmarried and
having a tiny private income. But only the talent, the commercial
potential of which he's so blithely unaware, will save even him from
being broken. Jerry Jemingham and Susie Dean are potential stars
and know it; they also know that talents equal to theirs have often
foundered in obscurity. Priestley was not writing a sociological or
political treatise. He was writing a novel. But a novel must hold a
mirror up to the times, it must give the reader the shock of recogni-
tion. The shock is as authentic today, because human nature hasn't
changed.

Over and above this, its continued popularity is due to the fact
that with it Priestley solved the problem of combining objective
narrative with subjective themes. The device of swooping down on
the Pennine Chain at the beginning and soaring away from it at the
end is the key. We do not merely look at the characters, we look
at England. The feeling is of space and freedom, the narrative surges
forward irresistibly. The lion in the path has been faced. He hasn't
been killed – one doesn't destroy such a beautiful beast. His vitality
has been absorbed, his energy harnessed. Priestley has entered
another stage of his development as an artist.

What is sad is that no one learned from his example. The straight
novelist (I wish there were a better term) remained in the subjective

groove. Some fifty years later he is still imprisoned in it, still looking inwards instead of outwards, still concentrating upon the private sensibilities of his characters. And his audience, partly because of the economics of publishing, has shrunk to vanishing-point. And the trouble isn't an excess of artistic integrity, but a lack of it, not overmuch concern with technique, but not enough. Or, to put it bluntly, simple laziness, the refusal to think deeply and seriously about his art, the refusal of challenges, the refusal to grow. A sidelight upon this is the complete failure even to learn from the example of *Ulysses*, which was regarded as being purely an interior exploration of character. But for Joyce, it was a day in the life of a capital city, and Dublin tram tickets and advertisement slogans were equally as important as the states of mind of Bloom and Dedalus.

I am not of course saying that Priestley is the same kind of writer as Joyce. I am saying that their attitude towards their art is the same, that they both understand that the world doesn't disappear when one's characters close their eyes, that the tree continues to be when there's no one about in the quad, that though quality mustn't be confused with quantity, a long book achieves more than a shorter book, just as a four-seater car holds twice as many as a two-seater. The dimensions of a novel matter as much as the dimensions of a painting: the greatest effects need the greatest space.

It should be emphasized that *The Good Companions* represents the beginning of a stage in Priestley's development, no more, no less. It does not represent the establishment of a pattern, the beginning of a series of variations on the same theme. For the theme of escape, of making a new life, would in 1930 have had even more appeal than in 1929. Nothing would have suited the public better than to have gone on the open road again with a new and even more delightful set of Good Companions.

But he wasn't interested in pleasing the public. He never had been. He was only interested in pleasing himself and doing the work. He was in the public eye now – more so perhaps than a writer of comparable stature would be today. His image, without the aid of TV or public relations, was virtually three-dimensional. 'Jack is pretty well unique in the world of writers,' Norman Collins says. 'It's a world in which gusto and bounce weren't exactly predominant. Physically he's very strong. He has a soccer player's build. He stands out vigorously with those broad shoulders and that heavy build – he's a big man ...' He was now at the height of his powers. He was past the dark years, past the years of struggle, past the years when merely to survive was a triumph. Literally, he was rejoicing in his almost superhuman physical and intellectual energy. He enjoyed life as few men do. 'Jack was enormously active,' Norman Collins says,

I've never known anyone so active. There never was a moment when he wasn't doing something. For example, as soon as he moved into his first Isle of Wight house he had a tennis court installed and indoors a billiards table and a ping-pong table. He even enjoyed his music energetically. He was the last of the pianola players. He took his pianola playing very seriously. He became like a man possessed, turning his head from side to side, giving it all he's got ... But he threw himself with equal energy into work and play. I remember at Highgate he told me that as soon as he was up he wanted to get on with his work. He didn't want to waste time with the ridiculous business of putting on trousers, shirt, jacket and so on. So he had a one-piece zipper suit made, lined with wool. Unfortunately it wasn't ventilated. So he ended up ankle-deep in his own sweat.

There is no trace of sweat in *Angel Pavement*, published in 1930. He was challenged by an idea and happily met the challenge. Its theme is the exact opposite of *The Good Companions*. It's about people whose lives will never change except for the worse, who have the possibility of a better life dangled invitingly before them for a brief while, only to have it snatched away again, to leave them worse off than before. It most emphatically isn't a Marxist novel, since Priestley isn't and never has been a Marxist, but it could be regarded as almost a documentary proof of the law of economic determinism, which states that our lives are exclusively shaped by our economic environment. And no one escapes to the open road. The action never leaves London. The characters are in a sense all prisoners of London. All that can sustain them in the end is dogged endurance and ordinary unromantic love – huddled together for warmth against the storm.

Farthing Hall had bought Priestley the time to write *The Good Companions*. And this in its turn bought him the time from then onwards to write exactly as he pleased, with no pressure upon him but the pressure of the work itself. (It has to date sold 473,403 copies in the UK hardback alone, excluding paperback editions, book-club editions, special editions and foreign translations. Including these the figure would be in the region of 4,000,000.) It is vital here to be meticulous in defining one's terms. Priestley from the beginning of his career as a professional writer had never written otherwise than how he pleased. A professional writer must be paid just as any other professional man must be paid. In any case, if what he has written isn't worth paying for it isn't worth writing. But if his motive in writing is solely to make money then the writing will be dead. Writing demands total commitment. Nevertheless a writer without large cash reserves and a continuing income meets his deadlines because of economic necessity. No matter how robust he may be, there are always lurking in his consciousness certain anxieties and insecurities which can eventually diminish the vitality which he needs for his work. Priestley has always met his deadlines, indeed often anticipated them; but there is all the difference in the world between meeting deadlines because you'll be in financial trouble if you don't and meeting deadlines purely because you're eager to get on with the next idea. The importance of money, as Somerset Maugham said, is that it releases one from the need to think about money.

All this is to make it clear that in writing *Angel Pavement* there were absolutely no commercial considerations. There is no wish-fulfilment here. If it has a message, it is that you can't win. Only the mysterious Mr James Golspie will win, coming from the Baltic at the beginning and leaving for South America at the end, leaving the small inlay and veneer firm of Twigg and Dersingham in ruins and in the process considerably enriching himself. Golspie is a nomadic predator, always moving on. The predators always win.

For they know how to choose their prey, they pick out the weakest in the herd. Twigg and Dersingham, when Golspie storms into its office at Angel Pavement, is already on the verge of insolvency.

'But honestly now, how are things going?' Mr Smeeth the cashier asks Mr Goath the firm's senior traveller. 'You've been on the North London round this time, haven't you? How's it going? Better than last time, eh?'

'No,' the other replied, with all the satisfaction of the confirmed pessimist. 'Worse.' He took off his bowler hat and for once examined it with the distaste it deserved. 'Much worse.' He goes on to amplify the statement, dismally fluent with the fluency of the born failure – 'Things are rotten. I've been in the trade thirty years and I've never known 'em worse ...'

The atmosphere of foreboding builds up, heightened by the intrusion of an itinerant traveller in office stationery:

'Good morning,' said a brisk but ingratiating voice. 'Any typewriter supplies? Ribbons, carbons, wax stencil sheets, brushes, rubbers?'

'Not this morning, thank you,' said Twig.

'Rubbers, brushes, stencil sheets, best-quality papers, carbons? Ribbons?'

'No, not this morning.'

'Well,' said the voice, a little less brisk and ingratiating now, 'if you should want any typewriter supplies any time, here's my card. Good-morning.'

'It's surprising, the number of these chaps we get round,' said Mr Smeeth, rather sadly, 'all trying to sell the same bits of things. If you bought anything, what would it amount to? A shilling or two, that's all. It beats me how they make anything out of it. Smart, well-dressed chaps too, some of them. I don't know how they do it, really I don't.'

They are seeing their future, like soldiers seeing their comrades fall in battle. The caller is apparently alive – *smart, well-dressed* – going through the motions of having a job, of earning a living, of being a useful member of society. But he is one not of the walking wounded but the walking dead. He is finished, he is empty, he's on the scrap-heap. He'd perhaps be better off if he gave up the struggle, let himself slide down to the bottom, to the fetid cosiness of the doss-house and the oblivion of meths. Then at least he'd have no further to go, he'd be spared the torment of a hundred disappointments a day and, perhaps worst of all, the burden of others' pity.

'"He's 'oping, that's what he's doing, just 'oping, like me," Mr Goath remarked grimly. "Only it doesn't run to spats with me. I'd better try 'em, then I might get a big order or two ..."' He relapses into self-pity, ruminating on the sad state of his inside, a shabby whisky-sodden man on the verge of old age, whose instincts tell him that he's on the way out.

What follows is a moment of truth almost frightening in its intensity. It would have no value if the ground had not been prepared, if Mr Golspie, Mrs Cross the cleaner, Stanley the office boy, Turgis the young clerk, Mr Smeeth the cashier, Miss Matfield the typist, and Mr Goath had not been fully described. We know what they look like, we know what sort of people they are. And, equally important, we know their background, we are authentically in Mr Golspie's ship steaming into the Port of London from the Baltic, we are authentically in the shabby little office in the shabby little street in the City of London. There is no question of set-pieces being slotted into the narrative: the characters are what they are because of their background and the background too is shaped in part by the characters. Mr Golspie doesn't shape the sea, but the sea is his element; distance is his province, he carries with him an aura of change and excitement.

His entrance is foreshadowed in the moment of truth, for in the moment of truth the trap is closing. Goath has virtually spelled it out: business isn't merely bad, it's getting worse. The traveller in office requisites has underlined it.

The room sank into a kind of mild sadness, rather like that of the atmosphere outside, where rich autumn had been bleached and deadened into a mere smokiness and gathering grey twilight, in which the occasional smell of a sodden leaf came like a remembrance of another world, as startling as a spent arrow from some battle still raging in the sun.

The faces of the three men, Mr Smeeth's grey oval, Goath's purple pulp, Turgis's tarnished youth, sank with the room, were half frozen into immobility, and seemed for a moment or two to be vacant, staring into nothing. Miss Matfield, who had risen from her table, saw it all for one queer second tangled with a whole jumble of deathly images: they were all under a spell, powerless to stir while the sky rained soot, dust poured from every crevice, and cobwebs wound about them ...

Time has stopped, the trap has closed. But this isn't the author's comment, a report from outside. Nor is it subjective, a description of conscious thought. It is what happens at that stage in the narrative, it is almost concrete and three-dimensional, no more to be described as conscious thought than is a crowd's panic in a burning building.

The passage has a terrible poignancy, it sticks in the memory as if it were one's own experience. A novel entirely composed of such passages – if it were possible to maintain emotion at that intensity – would not of course be a novel at all, but an attempt at a poem. A novel without such passages – and I don't believe that they can

43

be planned – would be dead, a narrative in monochrome, a narrative based on the proposition that only the exterior world is real, only the sensible and balanced and prosaic emotion is valid. And here, too, is compassion, the compassion which Gorky spoke of when he imagined Chekov looking at the muddle of human life, the sad and confused way in which most of us live, and saying: *My friends, you live very badly; it's a shame to live like that.* The compassion is implicit, never stated, and it is implicit throughout and is ours as much as Priestley's.

Miss Matfield breaks the spell by upsetting a box of paper fasteners and they're all back in what is called the real world again. Howard Dersingham, the principal of the firm, has arrived, and asks Smeeth for a statement of outstanding accounts. Something is in the air, trouble is on the way. But there isn't any question of the trouble being the consequence of capitalist exploitation. Howard Dersingham may technically be a capitalist and technically live on others' labour, and is indeed a kind of parasite. For Twigg and Dersingham produces nothing, handles nothing. It makes a profit or, rather, attempts to make a profit by acting as an agent between the makers of a product and the users of a product. Its profit is the difference between what the manufacturers of the veneers and inlay charge and what the furniture manufacturers will pay. And, as Mr Goath has gloomily pointed out, the furniture manufacturers, though furniture prices are higher than ever, want the veneers and inlays cheaper and cheaper. What is astounding – as I remember thinking when I first read the novel at the age of twenty – is that the furniture manufacturers don't themselves deal direct with the veneer and inlay manufacturers. This never occurs to Dersingham. It never in fact occurs to him to do anything constructive about the situation. He has never even considered that the whole basis of his business is precarious, he has never even considered trying some other kind of business. For he isn't really interested in business. All that he really cares about is being a gentleman.

None of this is stated directly. If it were, then we'd merely be given the author's opinion about the British class structure of the Thirties. We are in the first instance shown what sort of person Dersingham appears to be at first sight:

Seated at his table, looking through the morning letters, as he was now, Howard Brompton Dersingham might have been accepted as a typical specimen of the smart younger City men ... He looked too good for Angel Pavement, where business is merely business and a rather haphazard and dusty affair at that. He would not have seemed out of place in one of those skyscrapers filled with terrifically efficient and successful operatives and administratives, in those regions where business is not at all a haphazard and dusty affair and takes on a solemn air, even a mystical tinge, as if it really explained the universe ...

Another glance or two, however, would reveal the fact that he was only a rough, weakly unfinished sketch of the type. The hard-boiled eye, the chiselled nose, the severely controlled mouth, the masterful chin, all these were missing, and in their place were ordinary masculine English features, neither very good nor very bad, very strong nor very weak. Mr Dersingham was a year or two under forty, tallish, fairly well built but beginning to sag a little; his hair, which was now rapidly taking leave of him, was light brown, and his eyes light blue, and they neither sparkled nor pierced, but just regarded the world blandly and amiably; he had retained one of those short pruned moustaches that crept under the noses of so many subalterns during the War; and he looked clean, healthy, and kind, but a trifle flabby, and none too intelligent ...

The device of showing what Dersingham is not, the extended metaphor used, as it were, obliquely, gives an extra force to the description of Dersingham as he is. Without it what we would have would be merely a description of a typical middle-class Englishman with no glaring vices, no conspicuous virtues, and without a glimmer of vitality. In short, Dersingham is in himself a bore. He is also thoroughly decent. He hasn't even one real vice, one shameful obsession, to make him interesting. The problem is how to describe a boring person without being boring. In this instance, Priestley's extended metaphor is the only possible solution. It wouldn't have been possible if he'd been bound strictly by the camera-eye technique and not allowed himself the freedom to comment when necessary.

Dersingham, having examined the figures which Mr Smeeth has prepared for him, now asks Miss Matfield to call in Mr Smeeth and Goath:

'Will you just ask them to come in – and then – er – just carry on with something, eh?'

'Very well,' said Miss Matfield.

'Good!' said Mr Dersingham. He never felt sure how he ought to handle Miss Matfield, quite apart from the fact that she seemed to him a rather formidable sort of girl. Her father, he knew, was a doctor, only a doctor in the country now, miles from anywhere, but he had once played scrum half with the Alsatians. Ordering about the daughter of a scrum half with the Alsatians, just as if she were some ordinary little tuppeny-ha'penny typist, was a ticklish business. And that was why Mr Dersingham added 'Good!': it meant that he knew all about the surgery and the Alsatians.

Character, it has been said, is action. The lazy way to have written this passage would have been to have omitted the 'Good!' The passage would have been regarded simply as the means of bringing Smeeth and Goath into Dersingham's office and advancing the story into the next crisis. The camera-eye technique would have retained the 'Good!' but have permitted no comment upon Miss Matfield's father. What the comment does is to build up not only the character of Dersingham but to add to our knowledge of Miss Matfield. Information about the character mustn't be given the reader all as it were in one breath, but must emerge at the right moment in the course of the story, and as part of the story. (Incidentally, the last sentence in the above quotation is a perfect example of the proper use of that neglected punctuation mark, the colon.)

Dersingham, having called in Smeeth and Goath, explains to them that the firm must make cuts. 'The first thing, the very first thing, we've got to do is to reduce the overheads in this business.'

The phrase is very useful – it enables Dersingham for a while at least to act out the role of a keen and efficient businessman. But what it all boils down to in the end is that Turgis or Miss Matfield must be sacked. The decision is deferred and in effect left to Smeeth. If Dersingham were capable of making the decision instantly, and carrying it out instantly, then the business wouldn't be rapidly going downhill.

The ground is prepared for the entrance of Golspie. Change is coming to Twigg and Dersingham's. In even the smell of his cigar that change is foreshadowed. 'Its fumes seemed to turn the office into a dull little box and their duties into the most mechanical and trivial tasks. There was something rich and adventurous about the drifting cigar smoke. It unsettled them ...'

Golspie, although he's obviously about to try to sell Dersingham something, is completely at his ease. Middle-aged, of massive build, balding, with bushy eyebrows and a huge moustache, he isn't handsome, he isn't charming, but he has a tremendous insolent vitality. He asks Miss Matfield about the origin of the name Angel Pavement:

'No, I don't know,' she replied, with a hint of distaste in her tone ... 'And I don't care.'

'No, you don't care,' said Mr Golspie, bluff, hearty, and completely unabashed. 'I don't suppose you care tuppence about the whole concern. Why should you? I wouldn't if I were a good-looking girl, not tuppence.'

Miss Matfield looked up again, this time wearily, wrinkling various parts of her face. Then she brought to bear upon this intruder the full force of her contemptuous gaze, which would instantly have routed Turgin, Mr Smeeth or Mr Dersingham, and a great many people of her acquaintance. On this objectionable man it had no effect at all. He stared hard at her, and then smiled, or rather grinned broadly ...

Golspie has sent out a sexual message or may even be acknowledging a sexual message. He is a predator in more ways than one. But Miss Matfield will keep and there are in any case a lot of women in the world; he goes in to see Dersingham and Goath, the three of them go out, and at the end of the afternoon Dersingham, who obviously lunched well, phones Smeeth to tell him that Turgis and Miss Matfield are to stay, but Goath, if he comes in, must be sacked. Goath comes in, an extraordinary apparition, drunk to the verge of incoherence. 'I've finished wi' them. They finished wi' me. All over.'

And he disappears, still repeating his theme phrase, *thirty years in the trade*; a trade which we know, without being told, will now have finished with him. He is the predator's first victim. The viewpoint changes to Smeeth's and we follow him to his six-roomed home in Stoke Newington where he lives with his wife and son and daughter. What is depicted here is something even more difficult to depict than a boring mediocrity. Priestley here depicts a happy marriage. Mr Smeeth enjoys his job and has his own integrity, but he is essentially a limited and cautious man and perhaps too kind and gentle for his own good. He is a born worrier and, though he'd rather be happy, he'll never have the courage to be ecstatically, uproariously happy.

His wife is the opposite:

She still had a great quantity of untidy brown hair, a bright blue eye, rosy cheeks, and a ripe moist lip ... By temperament, however, she was a real child of London, a daughter of Cockaigne. She adored oysters, fish and chips, an occasional bottle of stout or glass of port, cheerful gossip, hospitality, noise, jokes, sales outings, comic songs, entertainment of any kind, in fact, the whole rattling and roaring, laughing and crying world of food and drink and bargaining and adventure and concupiscence ...

She is happy with Mr Smeeth. 'He had been her sweetheart, he was her husband; he had given her innumerable pleasures, had looked after her, had been patient with her, had always been fond of her; and she loved him and was proud of what seemed to be his cleverness ...' And he was happy with her. 'She still seemed to him an adorable person, at once incredible and delightful in the large, wilful, intriguing, mysterious mass of her feminity, the Woman among the almost indistinguishable crowd of mere women.'

Mr Smeeth is much more than a piece of office equipment. He is an individual and a vulnerable individual. He enjoys his work and gives Twigg and Dersingham good value for his £315 a year. (The approximate equivalent as I write would be £4,500.) What he does not enjoy, what is exacting a heavier and heavier toll, is the desperately insecure position of the firm. If it goes into liquidation then he knows that his chances of getting any job at all at his age are precisely nil. His home is his refuge, the rest area behind the firing line.

The next morning he is back into battle again. It's a wet grey day, Dersingham phones and says that he won't be in until late afternoon, everyone at the office is unsettled and depressed and disagreeable. And at lunch – poached egg on toast and a cup of coffee – Mr Smeeth is given an intimation of economic mortality.

The wet morning had perished outside, where there was even a faint glimpse of sunshine, but it had found a haven in this teashop, which seemed to be four hours behind the weather in the street, for it was all damp and steaming. Mr Smeeth was jammed into a corner with another regular patron, a man with a glass eye, bright blue and with such a fixed glare about it that the thing frightened you. Mr Smeeth was sitting at the same side as the glass eye, and as the owner of it ... never turned his head as he talked, the effect was disconcerting and rather horrible.

'Firm we've been doing business with,' said the man 'has come a nasty cropper – a ve-ery nasty cropper. Claridge and Molton – d'you know 'em? Oh, very nasty.'

'Is that so?' said Mr Smeeth politely, looking from his poached egg at the glaring blue eye and then looking away again. 'Don't think I know the firm.'

Relentlessly the man with the glass eye builds up the picture – 'One of the soundest concerns in the business eighteen months ago. Now it's properly in Queer Street ... Absolutely down the river ...' In short, the man with the glass eye, without knowing it, puts the boot in. We don't see him again. We don't hear of Claridge and Molton again. But we share Mr Smeeth's intimation of economic mortality, we too are hypnotized by that staring glass eye.

It could be argued that this passage is superfluous. We know from what has preceded that Mr Smeeth has good reason to fear losing his job. It might further be argued that it's a waste of effort to describe with so much care a character who's seen only once. But this is the strength of the long novel, this is why long novels, all other things being equal, are better than short novels. For the course of daily life isn't selective or logical. The staring glass eye of the man in the teashop does more to drive home to Mr Smeeth the danger of his losing his job than anything that Dersingham has said. It does more than the evidence of the figures which he's drawn up for Dersingham. Figures are not real even to an experienced book-keeper. The staring glass eye, the steamy teashop, the decline and fall of Claridge and Molton, are real, the moment has a nightmare intensity.

And then at five o'clock Mr Dersingham arrives, 'bursting in like a large pink bomb'. Golspie, who has the sole agency for veneers from the Baltic at prices up to fifty per cent lower than Twigg and Dersingham has been paying, is to lead or, rather, drive the firm out of the red into the black. But black is an inappropriate colour: the future is golden for Twigg and Dersingham and there is even to be a big rise for Mr Smeeth.

Dersingham doesn't, of course, ask himself why Golspie should come to him in the first place. He naturally thinks of Golspie as 'a terrible outsider'. It doesn't occur to him that there's anything odd about Golspie wanting his commission as soon as the veneers are delivered, without waiting until the account is settled. For Dersingham is an English gentleman before he's a businessman. He doesn't even know that, in the American phrase, there are no free lunches. He doesn't ask himself why Golspie won't wait to draw his commission until the accounts are finally settled. Dersingham is an innocent, living in a dream world. Golspie is a predator, living in the world as it really is.

And when Golspie and his daughter Lena dine at the Dersinghams, the dream world is revealed in all its dusty and doomed absurdity. The Dersinghams occupy a lower maisonette somewhere between Gloucester Road and Earl's Court Road. They have a cook and a maid, both thoroughly incompetent. Mrs Dersingham looks 'like thousands of other English wives in their earlier thirties, that is, fair, tired, bright, and sagging'. Her public fantasy is that her life is 'one exciting and multi-coloured whirl of people and events'. The reality is that most of the time she's bored, that the flat is ineptly designed, dark, and depressing, and that the whole area is rapidly going downhill.

The other guests are a typical assembly of English middle-class grotesques. There are Mr and Mrs Pearson, a middle-aged couple who have just retired from Singapore. They are stupid, boisterous, but not malignant. There is Miss Verever, 'a tall cadaverous virgin of forty-five', who is both stupid and malignant, and who has developed to a fine pitch the art of making everyone around her uncomfortable. And there are the Tropes – 'tall, cold, thin, and rather featureless'. Trope retains his wartime rank of Major, and what he imagines to be a military manner. They are also stupid, but expend so much energy in maintaining the glacial haughtiness appropriate to their class – or to be more accurate, the class they've placed themselves in – that they haven't enough left over to be malignant.

The soup is greasy and Miss Verever leaves most of hers. And during the fish course Golspie shakes Major Trope by preferring soccer to rugby:

'What, you a soccah man? Not this professional stuff? Don't tell me you like that.'

'What's the matter with it?'

'Oh, come now! I mean, you can't possibly – I mean, it's a dirty business, selling fellahs for money and so on, very unsporting.'

'I must say I agree, Trope,' said Mr Dersingham. 'Dashed unsporting business, I call it.'

'Oh certainly,' Major Trope continued, 'must be amateurs – love of the game. Play the game for its own sake, I say, and not as these fellahs do – for money. Can't possibly be a sportsman and play for money. Oh, dirty business, eh, Dersingham?'

Golspie is unmoved. 'We can't all be rich amachures. Let the chaps have their six or seven pounds a week. They earn it. If one lot of chaps can earn their living by telling us to be good every Sunday . . . why shouldn't another lot be paid to knock a ball about every Saturday, without all this talk of dirty business? It beats me. Unless it's snobbery. Lot o' snobbery about in this country. It pops up all the time.'

The predator is classless. He certainly doesn't believe in equality, much less the brotherhood of man. But as far as he's concerned the whole notion of being a gentleman and playing the game is a waste of time. He has no class. Indeed, he has no country. And he is absolutely self-possessed. He is entirely masculine, entirely forceful, the others are two-dimensional besides him, mere caricatures of human beings.

The maid, perhaps affected by all this, slips coming into the room and the entrée is ruined. But Mrs Pearson saves the meal from disaster by quickly preparing a huge mushroom omelette in its place. And Mrs Dersingham has gained a friend from the evening. Mrs Pearson may be stupid and boisterous but she's kind-hearted and resourceful. Whatever their faults, Empire-builders could cope with disasters. And Mrs Pearson is happy for the first time since her husband's retirement because now she's being of some use, not merely killing time.

Again a character seen only incidentally is brought to full life. When compared with Golspie the other guests are indeed two-dimensional; but they are not so to themselves. And another theme is taken up here, one which recurs throughout the novel and indeed throughout Priestley's work. This is, to put it very simply, that women, as far as all the things which really matter are concerned, are superior to men. They are wiser, they are kinder, they are nearer to earth. Mrs Pearson doesn't panic at the moment of crisis, she doesn't lose her temper: she miraculously produces the only thing which really matters, the huge smoking hot mushroom omelette.

At the dinner table Golspie and Trope are near to quarrelling and Dersingham feels himself to be in an awkward situation, not wishing to offend either. He mumbles that there's a lot to be said on both sides.

This doesn't calm down Major Trope:

'There may be ... but I don't like to hear a man continually running down his own country. Tastes diffah, I suppose. But I feel – well, it isn't done, that's all.'

'Time it was done then,' said Mr Golspie aggressively. 'Most of the people I meet here these days seem to be living in a fool's paradise –'

The predator is showing his contempt for his prey. And, stupid though Major Trope may be, he can't be expected to endure it. A real quarrel is averted by the unexpected entrance of Golspie's daughter Lena, who has come from Paris that day and has come to the Dersinghams purely on impulse. Lena is 'the complete attractive young female animal', as self-possessed as her father, with an accent which is not as much foreign as international. She is an international person, one of the Beautiful People before her time. She makes the other women seem awkward and boring frumps and the evening ends in total disaster and tears. For she is not only the complete attractive young female animal; she is a spoilt child.

She will make more trouble, and particularly for Turgis, the young man who is Mr Smeeth's junior. Turgis is a bachelor living in lodgings, bored with his job and frightened of losing it, bored with his leisure, and sustained only by the dream of love. He has no ambitions, no interests, no friends, no mental resources, no memories and, on three pounds seven shillings a week, hasn't even the means to buy the most obvious kinds of oblivion. But he wouldn't want them, he only wants love. And this dream, on the face of it an impossible one, is what gives his life its only purpose:

He knew that he had little to offer on the surface, was nothing to look at, nobody in particular, but he felt that inside he was different, he was wonderful, and that sooner or later a girl, a beautiful and passionate girl, caring nothing for the outside show, would recognize that difference, this wonder, within, would cry, 'Oh, it's you', and love would immediately follow. Then life would really begin ...

And Lena, to pass the time, without even the excuse of passion, amuses herself with him briefly, and then shatters the dream.

Miss Matfield is far more attractive as a woman than Turgis is as a man, has far more vitality and sense of purpose. But she is reaching the age where she can see only the alternatives of a loveless marriage or a lonely spinsterdom in a women's hotel. She almost succumbs to Golspie – he is almost certainly a crook, certainly not a gentleman, he is vulgar and flashy and overbearing, but he is a man, he makes things happen and, above all, he desires her and makes no bones about it.

Golspie makes his financial kill, and he and Lena leave by ship for Valparaiso. He has briefly transformed the lives of all at Twigg and Dersingham; they have, through him, been given the hope of prosperity, perhaps even of security. Now Dersingham will survive for a while on what's left of his capital and then will, like his employees, have to look for a job. What has actually happened is that Golspie has transferred a large sum of money from Dersingham's pocket to his. It's all within the law, but it wouldn't have been possible without Dersingham's greed and stupidity. Golspie will go on to make another killing: predators are never short of victims.

The story continues after the last sentence. That is, one feels that the lives of the characters continue, just as London continues. They will not cease to exist because this is the right moment to end their story, any more than London will cease to exist. Smeeth and Dersingham have their wives to share the struggle, and Turgis unexpectedly does find love. There is no indication that Miss Matfield will be otherwise than alone. In all likelihood Golspie has spoilt her for lesser men, certainly for the feeble young man whom we see pursuing her at the beginning.

Angel Pavement, like *The Good Companions*, was a best-seller and is still selling steadily. It can be argued that the reason for the popularity of the latter is that it is a fantasy of escape, of wish-fulfilment. But *Angel Pavement*, as I have tried to show, is the exact opposite of fantasy. It hasn't the least hint of sentimentality. It could even be said that to some extent Priestley has loaded the scales against his characters, that even in the late Twenties things weren't as bad as that, that in some respects people were better off than today. However that may be, what is proved by *Angel Pavement* seems to be that the general public loves the truth when it sees it. I cannot see any evidence of Priestley making the least compromise to public taste – or rather to what public taste is generally supposed to be.

On a personal note, I returned to *Angel Pavement* with a very real trepidation, not having read it again since 1940. I was aware of it scarcely existing as far as the consensus of British literary opinion was concerned. The consensus was simply that it was a non-book when compared with, for example, *A Passage to India, Ulysses*, or *Sons and Lovers*. It simply wasn't to be regarded seriously, it wasn't a novel at all, but a best-seller. If it were mentioned in any literary history it would be patronizingly categorized as middlebrow. It was as if there were some test which Priestley hadn't passed or some necessary professional qualification he didn't possess. (John O'Hara's position in the USA is, interestingly enough, very much the same.)

This feeling is of course purely subjective. There is no way of proving it except by pointing out how little has been written about Priestley in general and this novel in particular. My personal impression is that he hasn't been blacklisted by the literary pundits but whitelisted: it's as if he didn't exist.

This – still on a personal note – did not affect my judgement of *Angel Pavement*. What it somehow did was to leave me totally unprepared to face the fact that here was a genuinely committed novel. It isn't a propaganda novel. It offers no solutions to social problems, least of all political solutions. But it is a novel about human beings in society. It does not explicitly condemn that society. What it shows of the lives of those who live in that society is implicit condemnation of that society. The reverberations are still with me as I write. And so is my understanding – at this late age – of the reason for the Second World War. For the Dersinghams, the Smeeths, Turgis and Miss Matfield, and all like them, war would be a welcome release, an expansion of horizons, an end to insecurity, an end to loneliness. For when war comes they live in a society which has a use for them, considers each one important. This is what is not said in the novel, but it is there nevertheless. And when I look back to 1939 – though I was far from being in as miserable a position as Turgis – I can now remember my delight when war was declared. Any change was a change for the better.

There is another reverberation from *Angel Pavement*. It isn't, again, a literary one. It is important, because it's the reason why the novel isn't ultimately depressing. It is the simple realization that for the majority life is better now than it was then. The improvement is chiefly in material terms, it may not last, we all live under the shadow of the H-bomb, the changes have been made in the most wasteful and clumsy manner possible – the house burned down to roast the pig. There still are firms like Twigg and Dersingham, and still predators like Golspie (though Golspie will be in the public sector now), loneliness is still the curse of big cities, and alienation the curse of our whole society. But, looking forward, the Dersinghams, the Smeeths, Turgis and Miss Matfield – victims all – would see our society as a kind of paradise.

The novel that has such reverberations, that has more than a literary value, that grows during the years, that has something fresh to say to each generation, can only be regarded as a masterpiece. It would with another author be regarded as the culmination of his career. International reputations have been founded upon less. Perhaps it was too much for the literary establishment to handle; perhaps it still is.

4

The Crowded Stage

Priestley now had arrived as a novelist. *The Good Companions* and *Angel Pavement* could not be dismissed as essayist's novels. The days of financial struggle were over (*Angel Pavement* has to date sold 85,300 copies in the UK hardback alone). A large and comfortable niche was ready for him. As he says in *Margin Released*, he refused to occupy it:

I turned to fiction – and this also explains why I have attempted so many different things – because I had a lot of ideas that would not leave me in peace and because I could not resist the challenge. I had never really been encouraged to write anything – the West Riding, where I grew up, had a genius for discouragement as stony as its walls – and whenever I broke through, to be accepted as one kind of writer, I was given to understand that was about all I could do. I could write an essay but not a novel; I could write a novel but not a play.

The challenge was accepted, and the first original play, *Dangerous Corner*, was written in a week. This represents an extraordinary burst of creative activity, even for Priestley. It should, however, be borne in mind that most plays are written at great speed in one short period of sustained effort. The period must be unbroken and there should be no variation of pace. To a great extent the form carries the writer along, for no time has to be spent in making decisions about the length or the number of characters or the backgrounds. The unlimited freedom of the novel means an unlimited number of choices. The dramatist must, if his play is to have any chance of being produced, work to a fixed length, have no more than eight characters, and no more than one set. The play must be divided into three or two acts of roughly equal length and, though these acts may be divided into scenes, too many scenes lead to confusion and confusion leads to boredom and an empty theatre. The more complex the plot of the play, the greater the necessity for the sustained and uninterrupted effort, the greater the necessity for speed: the plot is the choreography for a dance, not the blueprint for a story. A novel may be read at any pace; and it may be read at a sitting or put down and taken up again at any time for as long as a reader chooses. A play is always seen at one sitting and its pace is the pace of the cast. Though there are exceptions to the rule, only speed in writing gives the plot a natural and inevitable flow, for only speed enables the writer to keep the plot in his head without going back and devising jerkily instead of creating smoothly: it's like riding the Wall of Death or, more prosaically, whirling a bucket of water round one's head and not spilling a drop.

About *Dangerous Corner* Priestley says in *Margin Released*:

> The play itself was a trick thing, in which time divided at the sound of a musical box ... It was so poorly received by the daily Press – 'This is Mr Priestley's first play and we don't mind if it's also his last': that kind of welcome – that there was talk on the Saturday of taking it off, after five performances. If it had been taken off that night, I doubt if the play would ever have been heard of again. But with more favourable Sunday night notices, especially from James Agate and Ivor Brown, it had a comfortable run, and six years later it was revived. It then became the most popular play I have ever written. I doubt if there is any country in the world possessing a playhouse that has not seen *Dangerous Corner*, or if any other play written during the last thirty years has had the same reception ...

The play is, in my opinion, rather more than 'a trick thing'. The trick itself, the dangerous corner, is a masterstroke, a memorable expression of a fact of human behaviour which everyone knows and understands but which always comes as the same violent shock. The title is glaringly obvious until one realizes that no one had thought of it before Priestley, that the glaringly obvious title was *The Sleeping Dog* (the title of the radio play which is being broadcast as the play begins) and that *Dangerous Corner*, with its reverberations of pain and death and terror, of being helplessly sucked into disaster, not only states the theme precisely but in a profoundly poetic and compressed way. It would be hardly possible to pack more into only two words; the phrase has passed into the language.

The setting – the drawing-room of the Caplans' house at Chantbury Close after dinner – conforms exactly to Priestley's theory:

I have spent a good many of my working hours devising means to conjure audiences away from the prevailing tradition, after persuading them, perhaps for the first half-hour of a play, that they were safely within its bounds. It is for this reason – and not so much for reasons of economy – that I have so often favoured the play in one set; so that having carefully put us all in a sensible and conventional sitting-room, I could then begin playing my own particular tricks, edging away from conventional realism...

The characters are all in evening-dress. They are Robert Caplan, 'in his early thirties and a good specimen', his wife Freda, 'a handsome and vivacious woman of about thirty', Betty Whitehouse, 'a very pretty young thing', Gordon, her husband, 'in his early twenties and an attractive if somewhat excitable youngster', Olwen Peel, 'a dark, distinguished creature, Freda's contemporary', Charles Trevor Stanton, 'about forty, with a studied and slightly sardonic manner', and Maud Mockridge, 'your own idea of what a smart middle-aged woman novelist should be'. Robert is the principal of the family publishing firm, Olwen an executive of the firm, and Gordon and Stanton his partners.

The women are waiting for the men to join them as the play begins, and have been listening to the radio.

Miss M: What did they call that play?
Olwen: *The Sleeping Dog.*
Miss M: Why the sleeping dog?
Betty: Because you had to let him lie.
Freda: Let who lie?
Betty: Well, they were all telling lies, weren't they? Or they had been ...

The conversation continues, lightly, casually, building up the picture of pleasant middle-class people, after a good dinner, all business associates and personal friends, civilized and eminently well-balanced, with nothing to hide.

There is an awkward moment when Miss Mockridge mentions Robert's brother Martin, who committed suicide a year ago in a cottage some twenty miles away. But it's all glossed over; the men join the ladies and, quite casually, the conversation turns back to *The Sleeping Dog*.

Olwen (*who has been thinking*): You know, I believe I understand that play now. The sleeping dog was the truth, do you see, and that man – the husband – insisted upon disturbing it.
Robert: He was quite right to disturb it.

Robert is, of course, 'a good specimen'. He's a decent and honest man and hates deceit. Stanton is older and more experienced.

Stanton: I think telling the truth is as dangerous as skidding round a corner at sixty.
Freda (*who is being either malicious or enigmatic*): But life's got a lot of dangerous corners – hasn't it, Charles?
Stanton (*a match for her or anybody else present*): It can have – if you don't choose your route well ...

And, quite unexpectedly, the dangerous corner is reached. It would never have been, of course, at the point when Miss Mockridge mentions Robert's dead brother Martin. It looms up suddenly when Freda offers cigarettes from a musical cigarette box. The musical cigarette box hasn't been, as it were, pointed out to us. For it isn't, like a gun, an object which can itself play a decisive part in the action. It's what its presence reveals about Freda's relationship to Martin. The mystery increases. There is talk of a missing five hundred pounds. Olwen is hiding something. Freda is hiding something. Gordon is becoming increasingly agitated. They preserve appearances until Miss Mockridge's car calls for her. Miss Mockridge herself has enjoyed the evening. Her novelist's instincts are awakened.

Freda (*aware of the irony of this*): Oh, must you really go?
Miss M: Yes, I really think I ought ... (*shaking hands with Freda*) Thank you so much. (*Shakes hands with Olwen*) It's been so delightful seeing you all again – such a charming group you make ...

But the others know that the story that will go the rounds emphatically won't describe them as a charming group. They are now in the dangerous corner, skidding at sixty, and before the evening ends the dead Martin, so amusing and charming and handsome, will have been revealed as cold and destructive and more than half-mad and the snug little circle will be in ruins, the prosperous firm split down the middle, the three adoring couples adoring no longer and more disaster on the way. But what we are shown is the use of the device of splitting time in two, thus showing what *might* have happened. No matter how well we know the play the device never ceases to have its effect, one never ceases to be freshly delighted at the perfect working-out of the intricate plot. The characters indeed are conventional, their sins, even the dead Martin's, not quite as shocking now as they were in 1932. What shocks us, what has ensured the international and continuing life of the play, is the revelation that in each of our lives a dangerous corner can be on the way, a musical cigarette box is about to be opened. We hope it won't happen to us but to see it happen to others gives an edge to life – and giving an edge to life is part of what the theatre is about.

What theatre is also about (explains Priestley in *Margin Released*) is the struggle to survive in a lunatic world ruled neither by business sense nor artistic sense:

In the circumstances of production in the English-speaking Theatre you are compelled to exist in an over-heated atmosphere of dazzling successes and shameful flops, you are a wonder man in October, a pretentious clown in March, you are in, you are out ...

It is this gaming-house atmosphere that makes serious work in the Theatre so difficult in the English-speaking countries. You feel you have one foot in the playhouse and the other in the Stock Exchange ... It was my suspicion and dislike of this atmosphere that kept me away from the Theatre until I knew my children's food and clothing could be paid for, and it was out of a desire to escape the worst effects, once I was working in the Theatre, that I formed my own production company.

With his agent, A. D. Peters, he took over the management of *Dangerous Corner*. If he had accepted the verdict of the original management – and if he had not been willing to risk his own money – then *Dangerous Corner* would have sunk without trace. There are no second chances in the theatre as there are in the world of books.

Priestley continued to be actively involved in management and production, eventually founding the London Mask Theatre with Michael MacOwan and Thane Parker. Writing as one who can be kept from his real work a whole day by a handful of business letters – I personally find this as astounding as his extraordinary productivity as a writer. For he was no mere figurehead; he would have never consented to be. He was a decision-maker, a risk-taker (which isn't the same thing as being a gambler), a worker. To be involved in management alone is a full-time job for lesser men. It's a burden under which they groan, as often as not succumbing to stomach ulcers and heart attacks and nervous breakdowns. Priestley shouldered it and carried on, in the seven years from 1932 writing four novels – *Faraway, Wonder Hero, The Doomsday Men*, and *Let the People Sing*. There were in addition thirteen plays – *Dangerous Corner, The Roundabout, Laburnum Grove, Eden End, Duet in Floodlight, Cornelius, Bees on the Boatdeck, Time and the Conways, I Have Been Here Before, People At Sea, When We Are Married, Music At Night*, and *Johnson Over Jordan*. There were also the books *English Journey, Midnight on the Desert, Rain upon Godshill*, several film scripts, and an uncounted number of lectures and newspaper articles. The plays alone would have been a full-time job in the period – indeed a life's work – for lesser men. There has been nothing like it before. Scott and Balzac were enormously industrious, but the bulk of their output was in one direction and their ventures into business were disastrous. Dickens dabbled in the theatre as a diversion, edited a magazine, and found it an increasingly insupportable burden, and burned himself out with his recitals. These three were giants but could not in this matter of diversity and energy approach Priestley. (This, I hasten to add, is not a literary judgement.)

There is also the matter of the diversity of the plays alone. With each play, Priestley explored fresh territory. He knew that to do otherwise, to stick to themes proved to be successful, was death to the writer. But this is merely negative, it implies a conscious and rather frantic search for new ideas. And he has never searched for ideas: 'If I have written a great deal, this is largely because I have always had ideas for work to lure me on and on. Not all these ideas were good; many were indifferent, some terrible. But I have never been without them ...'

61

Laburnum Grove, his third play, was the first of Priestley's plays to be presented in association with J. P. Mitchelhill at the Duchess Theatre. This was a play, as Priestley says, with which 'everything went right'. It it still very much alive, frequently performed by amateur and repertory companies, and recently was back in the West End with Arthur Lowe, a comic actor of genius, in the original Edmund Gwenn part. (I didn't see Edmund Gwenn in the stage play, but I did see him in the film version; and only Arthur Lowe could have followed him.) It is a play which is indeed quiet, solid, bourgeois. As with *Dangerous Corner*, the theme is firmly stated in the beginning. But there the resemblance ends. There is no melodrama, no violence, no villain. There is only the hero, George Radfern. '*He is a man about fifty with nothing remarkable about his appearance, though even at the first there should be a certain quiet assurance and authority visible beneath his easy manner. At this hour, he is very much the suburban householder at ease, wearing slippers and an old coat, and smoking his pipe ...*'

What is clear here in this description of George is the advance from *Dangerous Corner*. The descriptions of the characters in *Dangerous Corner* are descriptions of stock characters, as Priestley himself has said. George is a character in the round. One feels that one has met George, one feels that one likes him. One also feels, because of that quiet assurance, that there's more in him than meets the eye, that, above all, he isn't going to be boring. One feels that his cadging brother-in-law, Bernard Baxley, and his wife, have outstayed their welcome and that Bernard won't be lent the £450 which he's asking George for to set up an exclusive agency. And his daughter Elsie's young man, Harold Russ, who wants to borrow money to buy a second-hand car business: one feels that Harold also won't be lent the money and that he won't marry Elsie. But the last thing that George will do is to refuse Bernard and Harold the money outright. And the last thing he will do is to forbid Elsie to marry Harold.

Quite casually at supper George prepares the ground for his surprise:

> Baxley: This ham looks good, George.
> Radfern (*heartily*): I expect it is good, Bernard. You know, I don't
>   think that there's a meal in the week I enjoy more than Sunday
>   night supper, and I could tell you why. It's so peaceful.

Elsie (*with a touch of contempt*): You're all for being nice and peaceful, aren't you, Dad?

Radfern (*with quiet humility*): I'm afraid I am. I'm not like you folks.

Mrs Baxley: Don't count me with them. I don't want any adventures. I want to see a regular income arriving.

Harold: We'd all like that.

Radfern (*faintly sardonic*): Yes, I believe you would. But it's not so easy these days.

Baxley (*with loud complacency*): It's not so easy if you're straight. That's the point. I like money as much as the next man, but it's got to be clean money.

Harold (*in the same strain*): Of course. I'm just the same. Won't touch it if it isn't straight.

George listens, rather enjoying himself, as Bernard embroiders upon his theme, becoming positively lyrical in his praise of honesty. There is no menace; George isn't a menacing man. But as George listens – and the actor's art is as much to listen as to speak – he is a cat with a mouse and the mouse doesn't know that the cat's there:

Radfern: Well, I'm glad to hear you fellows feel like that. I used to feel it myself in the old days.

Elsie: What do you mean, Dad – in the old days?

Radfern: I mean, in the days when I used to be in the wholesale paper trade.

Baxley: But you're still in it, the wholesale paper trade.

Radfern: How do you know I am?

Baxley: I've always understood you were.

Radfern: Well, I'm not. Haven't been in it for several years.

Baxley: But the firm's there and the office –?

Radfern: Oh, I keep them going, but it's just a blind. Pass the mustard, will you, Elsie.

The key words in this last speech are the last six. They can't be cut, they aren't ornament. And George really wants the mustard. He's absolutely unconcerned about making the revelation which is on the way. He isn't breaking down and confessing. He's enjoying himself in the same quiet way that he enjoys his supper.

The revelation comes step by step:

Radfern: Oh, I'd struggled with the business ever since I came back from the war. Slaved at it. Then the slump came. More slaving. But

63

> we had a good little connection in the fine-quality trade. And
> somebody wanted that, a big firm. They made me an offer. I
> didn't like it or the chap who made it. I turned it down, so this
> big firm did me in – never mind how – but they did. They won
> all right. Clever chap that, he's been knighted since – the dirty
> swine.

This, of course, is Priestley the social critic. George is saying that
big business is theft, he is already justifying himself. It doesn't have
a political flavour, it's a natural enough thing for him to say, it doesn't
set the action awry, it isn't, in Stendhal's phrase, like a revolver-shot
at a concert. To be a social critic is not the same thing as to be a
propagandist. The play is strong enough to accommodate a certain
amount of social criticism.

George reveals that he is a crook. The others still don't believe
him. Still quietly enjoying his supper, he makes it clear that he's not
joking:

Radfern: Of course I mean it. Every penny that's come into this house for
the last few years has been dishonestly earned.
Baxley: My God!
Radfern: (coolly): Tainted money. You've eaten it and drunk it and it's
clothed you and housed you and taken you to the pictures and
sent you to the seaside. If I'd gone on trying to make an honest
living, I don't know where you'd have been now, Elsie. As it
is, look at us. So nicely off that Harold here – and your Uncle
Bernard here – are both hoping I'll lend them several hundred
pounds each, on very doubtful security.

He is here, in an oblique way, saying that Bernard and Harold
are thieves too since essentially what they want is to take someone
else's money without working for it. He goes on to tell them that
his particular form of crime is to forge and counterfeit bonds and
notes. 'One of the most serious crimes in the calendar, Elsie. You
see, the banks don't like it, and what the banks don't like must be
a serious crime nowadays, like blasphemy in the middle ages.'

Again there is the note of social criticism; but what George says
is completely natural for him to say under the circumstances. A
politically committed writer would have had George go on to pro-
pose giving the banks to the people – and in so doing would have

turned him into a figure of cardboard and hot air and lost his audience.

We are, of course, from the beginning on George's side. On the other side are the Baxleys, the free-loaders and self-invited guests, who have already borrowed £250 from him, his daughter's fiancé, who wishes to borrow an even larger sum, and, later, the rather frightening Inspector Stack. And there are the huge impersonal forces against him too – big business, the banks, and the State itself. The State stumbled into the depression which ruined George's firm, the State not only didn't punish the man who wrecked the firm but honoured him. George is the individual against the State, George is all of us, George is fighting the dragon. The dragon could, of course, point out that George's activities are, as he himself admits, a cause of inflation, and that the chief reason for forgery being punished with extreme severity always has been, not that the banks don't like it, but that it makes everyone suffer, particularly the poor. It isn't only big business and the banks that George is robbing. But this is to break the butterfly on the wheel: *Laburnum Grove* is a play and not a debate. And it has another side to it, the bloom on the butterfly's wings, so to speak. It is perhaps the most English of all Priestley's plays – as he says, 'It has not been as widely and successfully produced abroad as many of my other plays have.' It captures unforgettably the atmosphere of the English suburbs in late summer. George describes it with love:

Here's Shooters Green, one of North London's newest suburbs. Very clean, very respectable, bright as a new pin. Nice little shops in the High Street. *Yes, madam, shall I send it? Certainly, madam.* Tea-rooms, Picture Palaces. *Good morning, Mrs Robinson. Good evening, Mr Johnson.* And here's Laburnum Grove, one of its best roads, very quiet, very respectable, best type of semi-detached villas. *Ben Machree, Craig Y Don, Mon Repos.* All nations, you see. *Heather Brow* – though there isn't any heather for miles around. And us – *Ferndale.* Nice little houses. Nice people. Quiet, respectable. No scandals. No brokers' men. No screams in the night. Morris Oxfords, little green houses, wireless sets ...

The absurd names are the labels for private dreams, private kingdoms, the prosaic details compose the fleece in the clear mountain stream, catching the gold dust of poetry.

About *Eden End*, produced at the Duchess Theatre, London, in the autumn of 1934, Priestley says in the introduction to volume one of his plays:

It gave me great satisfaction to write it – and I can well remember now the exquisite summer evening when I completed the last act, the tender light of the dying day on my final page. I brooded for a long time over the people of this play and their lines, and then wrote it quickly and easily: and to my mind this is the way that plays ought to be written. The long brooding brings depth and richness; and the quick writing compels the whole mind, and not merely the front half of it, to work at the job.

It ran for over a hundred and fifty performances in London at a profit, it was taken up by the repertory and amateur companies and, best of all, 'the people who did like it found something more than an evening's entertainment in it, were caught and held, by the life that I had imagined, were moved as I had been moved; and no writer can reasonably ask more than that'.

If one were asked to summarize *Eden End* in one word, that word would be *Chekovian*. Or, given five more words, one might mention *A Month in the Country*. This doesn't mean that Priestley copied Chekov or Turgenev (he couldn't have copied *A Month in the Country* in 1934 in any case). It doesn't mean that *Eden End* could have been written by anyone else but Priestley. It means simply this: the characters are seen with loving kindness, with a certain gentle sadness. And this is still as if one had been asked to summarize quickly – for the play isn't sentimental, it isn't lachrymose, the characters are seen in the round, they are individuals and not stock types, not organizing their lives very well, but not necessarily predestined to enormous dooms. And, once again, the background – the Yorkshire Dales in 1912 – infuses the play with a peculiarly English poetry, unstudied, spontaneous, not manifested by any set-pieces.

The set is the sitting-room of Dr Kirby's house, Eden End – '*a comfortable, well-worn room, furnished in the style of an earlier period*'. Kirby is a hard-working GP, beginning to have trouble with his health. He has a son, Wilfred, in his early twenties, home on leave from his job with the British West African Company, a rather weak young man who has not yet learned the hard facts of Empire; two daughters, Lilian, in her late twenties, and Stella, in her late thirties. Lilian is well on her way to being the unmarried daughter fated to stay at home and look after Daddy – though Daddy is not the sort of man who would ever ask for anyone else to sacrifice themselves on his behalf. Kirby is a good man. The goodness *does* shine through and this is the great test of a writer – and of an actor. Villainy is easy. Stella is an actress now on tour abroad, a glamorous figure living in a different world, remembered with awe by the old nurse Sarah as a different order of being from her sister, of the family but of royal blood, remembered like a song by a great singer, transforming life when remembered. Lilian is friendly with Geoffrey Farrant, a former admirer of Stella's. Geoffrey is an ex-regular officer in his late thirties, a quiet and decent man, invalided out of the army after active service in the Boer War, quite happy hunting and shooting and looking after his estate.

Stella arrives, completely unexpectedly. She has come on pure impulse. 'I couldn't just write. I think I was afraid to. Either I had to stay away or come, just like this, with a rush. Don't you understand?' They do understand. If they don't understand why she hasn't been to see them once in the nine years she's been away, why she didn't come home to see them when her mother died six years ago, they don't say so.

And the enchantment and the glamour return to Eden End. It isn't quite like, to adapt what Somerset Maugham said of Ibsen, a stranger coming into a cosy and fuggy room, and opening all the windows with the result that everybody catches their death of cold. But it's near enough. And there's the complication of Stella's separated husband, Charles Appelby, a hard-drinking actor who has already begun to slide downhill – if indeed he may ever have been said to have climbed. (This was the part in the original played by Ralph Richardson; it was the beginning of his association with Priestley and the true beginning of his career.) Stella and Charles create a disturbance, they disrupt the smooth surface of life, but do no great harm, do no more than spoil a few dreams. Eden End will continue, and Stella and Charles will try again. The world of tenth-rate repertory, of cheap boarding-houses and constant insecurity, is a shabby one but it's the only world in which they can live. Stella will not return to Eden

End. Sarah, who began the play, the old nurse who loves Stella as a mother loves her child, who loves, expecting nothing, says goodbye to her:

Sarah: He's not a bad sort for an actor chap, though. I'll bet he takes a bit o' watching. But you look after him, love. He's nowt but a big daft lad – like 'em all.

Stella (*whispering*): Oh, Sarah, I don't know what to say. There aren't any words.

Sarah: Nay, love. Nay, little love. (*fondling her face*) And don't catch cold when you're coming out o' the theatres. (*very softly*) I'm an old woman now, a'most past my time. Happen I shan't see you again.

Stella (*crying*): Yes, you will. You must.

Sarah: Oh, I'll see you sometime. There's a better place than this, love.

Why do those last words of Sarah move us so much? Because she believes them as she believes that the sun will rise in the east in the morning. Because she is not frightened of death and so rises above being merely an ageing body, rises above the materialistic definition of a human being – so much water, a handful or so of chemicals, a machine made of quickly perishable materials, an electric light bulb which will burn itself out. There will be a better place, and those who know how to love will find it. That is part of the theme of *Eden End* and one of the reasons why Priestley had 'a special tenderness' for it.

There is a sad postscript to *Eden End*. The first three of Priestley's plays to be produced in New York had not been successful. It was suggested that he personally supervise the production of *Eden End* in 1935.

I had high hopes of it, partly because I understood that there was more demand for intelligence and sincerity in the Theatre in New York than in London, and also because a number of Americans connected with the Theatre had seen it in London and had been enthusiastic about it. On the other hand, I was a stranger on Broadway and this was not an easy play to do, and so I knew that I was in for trouble.

His instincts were right. The weather was unseasonably warm – 'a clammy Indian summer'. He had to form a syndicate to produce the play, and discovered through bitter experience that the world of the theatre was in an even more lunatic state of chaos in New York than in London. And the play, in the American sense of the phrase, did a bomb. This venture to New York had been, in short, a complete waste of time.

One feels completely bewildered that he should have undertaken it in the first place. The tremendous output one understands, just as one understands the Niagara Falls. It would not have been possible to Priestley to have limited his output at any time, no matter how theoretically desirable it may have been. Once he conceived an idea, it would have physically pained him not to give it form and substance. And one can understand the desire to supervise the production of a play which meant so much to him. But one cannot understand the venture into the world of business and, though it scarcely matters now, one is saddened at the waste of precious creative energy. All creative energy is precious, however great the amount which one possesses.

Priestley returned to the ranch in Arizona where his wife and family were spending the winter. This was their second stay in Arizona, where they had originally gone for the sake of his wife's health: 'One of us had been ordered by her doctor to keep well away from the damp, cold, and fog that regularly besiege Britain from November to March ... Our chosen district ... has the best winter climate in the world.' It had something more. Priestley felt at home there, he could work there. And in Arizona there was still some of the spirit of the American West – however imperfectly, the spirit of democracy still manifested itself, basically society was healthy. And then there was the incredible beauty – if that wasn't too pale a word – of Arizona. 'Arizona really is a wonderland. You ought to enter it by floating down a rabbit-hole ... It is filled with marvels ... There is about the whole state a suggestion of the Arabian nights ...'

Healthy flesh heals quickly. Priestley went to work in the little shack, well away from the main ranch buildings, which had been built for him with extraordinary speed. (Or, as he said, with what seemed to a European to be extraordinary speed.) The result was a novel set in London, *They Walk in the City*. Wryly, Priestley observed afterwards that the reviewers had commented upon the novel's 'brilliant reporting'. But he had in fact, as he says in *Midnight on The Desert*,

not a single note. I had to remember and invent the London of my story
... A man in Arizona who attempts to describe, with some wealth of detail, what it feels like to be a waitress or a parlourmaid in London, using not one single note, may be a good, bad or indifferent novelist, but he will certainly not be much of a reporter. He has removed himself far from the scene; he has not prepared himself to describe it; and only by a fairly violent use of his imagination can he identify himself with characters so entirely different from himself. If this is reporting, then I no longer understand the English language.

He also visited Hollywood to work on various screen plays. His memories of Hollywood are vivid enough – they are all there in *Midnight on the Desert* – but he is oddly reticent about the screenplays. (He actually insisted that his name be left off the credits.) And, what also is strange about this period, he didn't make use of the background of Hollywood in any of his novels. Admittedly, there is no sort of obligation upon any writer to use absolutely everything he has seen and experienced. And he well may use it at a remove, he well may use it as the basis for something which on the surface appears entirely different. A mystery remains. But a clue may be found in *Midnight on the Desert*.

Before he and his family went to the Arizona ranch they spent two or three weeks at a guest ranch near Victorville in the Mohave Desert in California:

Most of the other guests there were from Hollywood, directors and actors and their wives who wanted a short rest, or had been ordered to take a child away from the coast for a time. These were not the stars, not the big names, but the front-line troops, the NCOs and the junior officers, those who did the real work in the film industry.

The one who taught Priestley the most about Hollywood was an assistant director whose wife and daughter had been sent to the ranch by the doctor and who commuted from Hollywood:

He was a short thick-set chap in his early forties, very tough, but friendly and likeable and immensely entertaining ... very masculine, courageous, kind-hearted, devoted to his womenfolk and his pals, sentimental about a few things; but entirely disillusioned about or indifferent to a great many other things ...

Priestley knew America. He knew, to his cost, the America of Broadway, the theatrical America. He knew the America of the universities and the luncheon clubs. He knew, to his delight, the Arizonian America, the generous and energetic America, the America where democracy was still a word of power. But the assistant director told him about an America he did not know:

He did not belong to it himself. It is a world below that agreeable surface of genial acquaintances, excellent travel arrangements, and scrupulous hygiene, which the visitor knows. It is a world partly revealed by the newspapers, a world of racketeers and grafters, gunmen and pimps and molls, in which money is everything and the law and ordinary human decency are nothing, the police seem little better than a uniformed gang, millionaires are jealous and murderous Caliphs, the frame-up is a neat device for embarrassing the other fellow, and everybody and everything have their price. It is not a tropical underworld of hot blood and passion, of people too barbaric for the bourgeois virtues. It is a chilly, grey, cellar-like, fungus world of greed, calculated violence and a cold sensuality ... honour and decency and affection do not seem to have rotted there; they would appear to have never existed. Its inhabitants are so many talking wolves ...

This world, of course, we now all know well. At the time that Priestley first heard of it writers like Hammett and Burnett had, as he said, already begun to chronicle it. Later Raymond Chandler – whose talents Priestley early recognized – explored it further. Hollywood was deeply involved in it. The world of organized crime was – *is*, one should say – only part of it. As Priestley says, 'You could show it flourishing without a single trigger being pulled.' It is in fact the world of positive evil. And what Priestley unconsciously reveals in his reaction to it is the enormous and unbridgeable gap between the pre-1914 world and the post-1914 world. This is necessarily a gross over-simplification, but the 1914 War was not a conflict between good and evil. The Kaiser and Franz-Josef – again to grossly over-simplify – each thought that they represented good. It was a contest of innocents. The fighting men were innocents. They had grown up in a world where everything was measurably improving

71

almost day by day. In that world there was a ramshackle class system, an unjust class system, all kinds of preventable suffering. But the cause was intellectual laziness, stupidity, lack of imagination, short-sighted greed, not a deliberate will to evil. Illusion was the name of the game. And the illusions were being shifted, the reforms were being made, those were the true days of hope.

And what Priestley gained from that world was an unshakeable inner strength, an essential decency and normality and sanity. Toughness would be the wrong word; it implies callousness. Wholesomeness is nearer: it is as if there was no sickness in his psyche, as if he had an extra ration of spiritual white corpuscles to heal his wounds quickly. Everything has to be paid for. The one weakness of his work is the failure to understand evil. The generations after him grew up understanding evil. It was part of the air they breathed. The only hope that anyone of my generation ever seriously entertains is that there might be a faint chance of, in Kingsley Amis's words, preventing things from getting worse. Even though the Second World War was essentially a contest between good and evil, my generation went into it without the comfort of illusions. Our fathers had rid us of them.

So Priestley never used Hollywood or, indeed, his experiences of the film world. His hero, Gregory Dawson, in the novel *Bright Day* is a film writer with long experience of Hollywood, but he is curiously untouched by it. He worked there, must have been enthralled as a craftsman by the glittering technical expertise of the film industry, but he rejected it. It was too alien, too unreal. And no good came out of it, not even money – 'Thus I noticed once more that the easy big money of Hollywood seemed in most people's hands – and I was sure that mine would be amongst them – to turn into fairy gold which is glittering heavy metal one moment and dead leaves the next ...' Unlike the hero of Evelyn Waugh's *The Loved One* he didn't carry away a huge lump of raw material, of primal experience to be shaped into a work of art. He was right to obey his own instincts, to listen to his own daemon, his sensible daemon: but to this day one can't help regretting that he didn't use this experience, that he didn't explore the other America that he had mapped out for him at Victorville.

Back in Arizona he discovered P. D. Ouspensky's *New Model of the Universe* and began to explore the problem of Time. He was not looking for a subject. He has never had to look for subjects; they have rather looked for him. He found himself a lonely traveller. Everyone he met accepted the conventional theory of Time. 'Apparently it was all dull and plain sailing to them. Time went on and on, you couldn't stop it, and that was that. They were blankly incurious . . .' Priestley was devouringly curious. He hadn't accepted conventional Christianity, but he hadn't ever accepted conventional materialism either. He read and he thought, he went on to consider further the theories of J. W. Dunne and Professor Rhine, and slowly and with gathering excitement made his way forward. He was about to take his work into a new phase.

It is impossible to read his account of his exploration of the mystery of Time without sharing that excitement. What he was doing was the job that the philosophers shirked. They still shirk it, in fact: all that modern philosophy amounts to is a series of disputes about linguistics conducted in a jargon incomprehensible to the majority. He doesn't write down to his readers: he pays them the compliment of treating them as adults. Adults are willing to take the time and the trouble to learn the truth. And adults hunger for the truth, hunger for intellectual effort, something to get their teeth into. There is also the matter of duty, the matter of living for something outside of oneself. Art begins, in the words of W. B. Yeats, as 'a lonely impulse of delight'. And so, too, thought begins. Priestley's reading had led him into the exploration of Time. He is a great reader; with him reading is as creative an act as writing. But the delight is to be shared – sharing is an inseparable part of the creative process.

Priestley's thoughts on Time eventually took dramatic shape in *I Have Been Here Before*, which was first produced at the Royalty Theatre, London, in the autumn of 1937. There were, in between, several other plays, *Midnight on the Desert*, and a trip to Egypt and the Sudan. And what this summary does not take into account is that he was actively involved in the production of the plays – something which in itself would have been enough for lesser men. Yet, though he admits to having always been driven by the 'puritan work ethic' he was in no sense a recluse, a work machine. He led a full social life, he had many friends, he was a good husband and father. His wife said of him at this time: 'Jack is not in the least temperamental. If a meal's late it doesn't matter. And he doesn't swear if he loses a cuff-button. He's wonderful with the children. He'd spend all his time playing with them if I didn't make him work. He improvises music for their little plays and has a beautiful time with them.'

This, of course, was another source of strength and refreshment as were his houses in Highgate Village and the Isle of Wight. He lived in great style with two beautiful houses and servants to run them smoothly; the puritan ethic applied chiefly to work. All this is in one sense irrelevant. Every penny he had was earned by his own work, and not one penny by financial juggling or exploitation of others. (It is worth commenting upon that no one professionally connected with authorship, particularly the printers, can be said to be underpaid.) He enjoyed every material comfort and it was right and just that he should do so. There was no contradiction between his life style and his description of his beliefs as 'strongly left'. He was also 'definitely non-Marxist': he hoped for a society in which there was a level beneath which no one would fall but above that no limits to the heights to which hard work and enterprise could take one.

His working day is detailed in *Instead of the Trees*:

> I am down to breakfast at nine ... and then, after dictating a few letters ... I go upstairs to shave and dress, usually about 10.30. I come down and work until about 12.50 ... I take a short walk in the afternoon ... and then I read or do a little work until tea. I am at work again, roughly between 5.30 and 6.30 – only an hour but an hour of actual writing, and not thinking about writing. (I do that at teatime.) Then I go up for a leisurely shower and a change of clothes ... Bed about 11.30. Read until about one o'clock, sometimes later ...

This roughly has always been the pattern, except that the little walk once would have been an energetic game of tennis or squash and the little work a lot of work. His guests have often spoken of the almost frightening sound of the typewriter from his study in the morning and afternoon, continuous and untiring, the sound of creation.

I Have Been Here Before, unlike so many of his other plays, did not come easily. There were three drafts, the final draft being written in a nursing-home in Italy. It lacks the flow, the irresistible assurance, of the plays like *Eden End* which were written at great speed after long brooding. Priestley says of it: 'I rewrote it several times, chiefly because it was very difficult to explain Ouspensky's theory of recurrence on which the action was based.' One would disagree with him here. Undoubtedly he seems to have looked at the theme first and the characters second, with the effect that recurrence dominates the characters. But at the heart of the theory of recurrence is choice. We have been here before, all of us, but when we go there again, we have a choice as to where we go next. It is not quite the same as the Eastern concept of reincarnation. It might even be regarded as stemming from the fundamental Christian doctrine of free will. Aquinas or Kierkegaard would have accepted it though obviously Calvin wouldn't. This matter of choice ('If we know and then make the effort, we can change our lives') is made abundantly clear in the play. Somehow or other, however, one has the feeling that the choice is inevitable and can't be changed, that it was the author's choice and not the choice of the characters.

It is futile to speculate over what might have been, and impertinent for a minor artist to criticize a major one. But one can't help feeling regret that Priestley didn't give himself more time for brooding, that what he describes as the three-ring circus – books, the theatre, journalism and public speaking – made such heavy demands. There are limits even to a giant's energy.

All this aside, the play survives to this day, and has been frequently produced here and on the Continent. The sheer interest of the theme – and its essential hopefulness – have ensured its enduring appeal; and, it should be added, its essential stageworthiness. There is one set and six characters and no fancy effects, and it is, above all, a play and not a debate.

The time is June. The setting is the sitting-room of an inn in the Yorkshire Dales. At the opening the landlord, Sam Shipley, 'a stout, humorous, contented Yorkshireman in his sixties', is expecting three women teachers from Manchester as his guests. A young headmaster, Oliver Farrant, is already a guest at the inn. Oliver is a highly intelligent and radical young man who has come to the Dales to recover from a near-nervous breakdown. Dr Gortler enters.

In the empty room we hear the clock ticking. A moment's pause. Then there is a quiet knocking on the outer door and it opens slowly, and Dr Gortler enters. The clock chimes. He is a man about sixty, in well-worn darkish clothes of a foreign cut. He has a slight foreign accent, and speaks with precision. Although his appearance and manner suggest the quiet detached scholar, he has a good deal of assurance and authority. He looks about him with eager interest and curiosity, and when he has taken the room in, consults a small notebook, as if comparing its appearance with some notes there. Finally he nods. Sam now returns, wearing his coat. The two men look at one another for a moment.

Every action here is significant. The art of the actor, as I have said before, means far more than the speaking of lines. Gortler's notebook is particularly important. Indeed, it could even be said that the battle for the audience's attention is won or lost here. If the notebook doesn't register itself, then the finale of the play will be muted. And the whole theme of the play is stated in this entrance, it is a kind of prologue. Dr Gortler asks about the guests who are arriving that weekend: 'Two of them – perhaps – are married people – the man older than his wife – he might be rich – and then – perhaps – a younger man?'

He's told about the three teachers from Manchester, and exits obviously puzzled, saying that this must be the wrong year. But the three teachers cancel their visit and Walter and Janet Ormund, who exactly fit his description, unexpectedly phone up to book two rooms for the weekend. Dr Gortler reappears and books a room for the weekend. Sally, Sam's widowed daughter, isn't happy about Dr Gortler. She senses trouble, she senses disturbance, she senses some sort of threat to her peace of mind.

When the Ormunds appear it instantly becomes evident that Ormund is a deeply unhappy man, using work – and whisky – as drugs in an attempt to dull the pain. It's also evident that his marriage is to all intents and purposes over. He and Janet are civilized and decent people, they're doing their best to arrive at some sort of working arrangement but there's nothing there, bitterness keeps breaking in.

The tension accumulates. When Oliver meets Dr Gortler he feels that he has met him before. When the Ormunds meet Dr Gortler, Janet suddenly finds herself feeling that she has been to the inn before, that she's had the same conversation with Dr Gortler:

Dr Gortler: Mrs Ormund, I am a student – a very old one now. Sometimes we students do not seem to have very good manners. I do not wish you to think I am – inquisitive, impertinent.

Janet (*with a slight smile*): It didn't occur to me that you were – or might be.

Dr Gortler: Lately I have been enlarging my studies – to include the human mind. So I go about asking questions.

Janet: If this means you want to ask me some questions, you can. But I don't think you'd find me much use. I've always thought the psycho-analysts monstrously exaggerated everything. I can't believe that all the little fears and fancies one has are of any real interest or value.

Dr Gortler: Even a few years ago, I would have agreed with you. But now I see that we do not understand ourselves, the nature of our lives. What seems to happen continually just outside the edge of our attention – the little fears and fancies, as you call them – may be all-important because they belong to a profounder reality, like the vague sounds of the city outside that we hear sometimes inside a theatre.

Janet: Oh! (*She stares at him, almost terrified*)

Dr Gortler: What is it?

Janet (*hesitantly and with wonder*): You see ...suddenly I felt ... I could have sworn ... you'd said all that to me before ... You and I – sitting, talking, like this ... and then you said 'because they belong ... to a profounder reality ... like the sounds of the city ... we hear sometimes inside a theatre ...' (*Dismisses the mood, then hastily*) I'm so sorry. I must be tired.

And Ormund is almost instantly disturbed by Gortler. It has transpired that Sally's son is a pupil at Oliver's school, that Ormund is a governor and important benefactor of the school, that Ormund, in the face of opposition and without seeing him, was responsible for Oliver being appointed headmaster, and that Sally and her father are shareholders in Ormund's firm. Sally is deeply suspicious of Gortler. 'Why should he come here looking for you?' she asks.

Ormund apologizes, but Sally sees her suspicions being confirmed – 'Why should he come here looking for you?' she asks Ormund.

Ormund (*puzzled*): For me?
Sally: No, for you three.

> (*This linking of the three of them together – for the first time – has its immediate effect, as if it chimed with some deep obscure feeling each of them knew. There is a pause, before Sally resumes.*)

> He comes here – looking about him – and when I tell him we've no room to spare because I'm expecting three visitors – he looks at me and asks if two of 'em are a married couple with the man older than his wife, and the other a younger man. And when I say No, we're expecting three ladies from Manchester, he seems disappointed and says something about it being the wrong year. So off he goes, and then the three ladies say they can't come, and you ring up for rooms, and when he comes back, there's a room for him too, and you're all here, and it's just what he expected.

Sally leaves, Ormund takes some papers from his brief-case, Oliver returns to his book. Janet is still thinking about what Sally has said. Ormund reassures her. 'We're all three a bit off our heads.' Farrant has been overworking. He himself has been 'half-dotty' for years, and Janet is 'always longing for marvels and miracles'. Janet is reassured and goes off to bed. Ormund and Farrant chat about the book, *New Pathways in Science*, which Farrant has been reading. Ormund cracks for a moment. 'What are we supposed to be doing here? What is it all about?' He recovers himself. Farrant goes off to bed, and Ormund is left working on his papers. He seems unable to apply himself to the job: he gets up, and in so doing breaks his fountain-pen in two.

And so, all in the first act, which covers the first day, the theme is stated, we are introduced to the characters. Well-made plays in the accepted sense of trite and conventional plays are exactly what Priestley has never written and has never wanted to write. But a well-made play in the literal sense is exactly what the play is. This first act is exposition and more than exposition; the characters react instantly as soon as they are put together. Janet and Oliver succumb to a *coup de foudre* and are on the verge of utter catastrophe; Ormund drives himself to the point of death, and in a way, against all expectation, takes the right way, the way of acceptance:

> The serener heart finds pure
> All that can happen to us.

These lines of Rilke's are not quoted in the play but, as it reaches its climax, they would not be out of place there. 'This play,' Priestley says, 'is an excellent example of the stealthy edging away from naturalism noted earlier. Thus many of the speeches in the third act are far removed from conventional realistic dialogue, and yet nobody commented upon the fact.'

Late in the day that omission may now be rectified simply by asking the reader to examine the following from the third act:

Dr Gortler: What has happened before – many times perhaps – will probably happen again. That is why some people can prophesy what is to happen. They do not see the future, as they think, but the past, what has happened before. But something new may happen. You may have brought your wife here for this holiday over and over again. She may have met Farrant here over and over again. But you and I have not talked here before. This is new. This may be one of those great moments of our lives.

Ormund: And which are they?

Dr Gortler (*impressively*): When a soul can make a fateful decision. I see this as such a moment for you, Ormund. You can return to the old dark circle of existence, dying endless deaths, or you can break the spell and swing out into new life.

Ormund (*after a pause, staring at Dr Gortler, then with a certain breadth and nobility of manner*): New life! I wish I could believe that. They've never told me yet about a God so generous and noble and wise that he won't allow a few decisions that we make in our ignorance, haste and bewilderment to settle our fate for ever. Why should this poor improvisation be our whole existence? Why should this great theatre of suns and moons and starlight have been created for the first pitiful charade we can contrive?

The achievement here is that this is not fine language for the sake of fine language. From the only acceptable testing-ground, the stage, the words ring true. The characters have reached a climax in their lives, they are taken out of themselves, they are taken out of the commonplace. They are climbing, and we climb with them. At this climax in their lives what would rob the play of all its force, what would be completely unnatural and artificial, would be conventional realistic dialogue.

Time and the Conways, produced in London at the Duchess Theatre in August 1937, was written quickly and joyously, according to Priestley in *Rain Upon Godshill*, and was produced and afterwards printed, with virtually no revision:

> The idea was not the usual possible good idea one jots down in a notebook and then leaves for a year or two. It excited me at once and I had to begin sketching out the general action of the play. I needed some 'period' details for these scenes; but I could not wait until we returned to London, where I could do my little bit of research, so I left the two 1919 acts and plunged boldly into the contemporary one, Act Two. With almost no preparation, without any of the usual brooding and note-taking, I wrote this Act Two of *Time and the Conways* at full speed ... Page after page, scene after scene, went off effortlessly, with hardly a correction in my typescript. I did not stay up late at night, drink strong coffee, put wet towels on my head; I kept a bank clerk's hours and almost behaved like one; and yet within two days I had almost finished this long and complicated act ...

The play is naturally classified by him as a Time play but in one sense it is not a Time play at all. The *if* game is a dangerous and a foolish game: but if Priestley had never read Ouspensky and Dunne, if indeed Ouspensky and Dunne had never existed, then the play could still have been written just as it stands. The action of the play can be detailed very briefly. The time of Act One is an autumn evening in 1919, the time of Act Two is an autumn evening in 1937, the time of Act Three is continuous with Act One in 1919. The setting is the same throughout: '*One of those nondescript rooms, used by the family far more than the drawing-room is, and variously called the Back Room, the Morning Room, the School-room, the Nursery, the Blue, Brown or Red Room.*'

The room is, in short, lived-in, it is a real room in a real house, not a stage set. It is almost superfluous to state in the stage directions that the house is a detached villa in a prosperous suburb of a manufacturing town. For we know, watching the play, that what takes place outside the sitting-room actually does take place, that there actually are other rooms beyond the sitting-room, that the rooms make up the house, that there is a town outside the house. It's as if there were a bigger play, taking in every room in the house, taking in the town around it, it's as if everything we are told about what happened between 1919 and 1937 were contained within that play. Every literary form has its limitations; the limitation of the stage play is that it can't realistically show all the action. The players have to put over a kind of confidence trick, make us see and hear what we actually haven't seen and heard. In the average play, the well-made play in the derogatory sense, at best we admire the writer's cleverness, and suspend our disbelief as a reward. With *Time and the Conways* there are no confidence tricks. The characters are telling us what happened to them, they are reporting reality.

To say that *Time and the Conways* is not in one sense a Time play is merely to say that it's essentially different from *I Have Been Here Before*. In the latter the dramatist is to a great extent dominated by the theorist, the conscious half of the brain is in charge. *Time and the Conways* was written at the deepest level of the brain, it was, as it were, finished before he wrote it. To say that he wrote it is, of course, inaccurate. It would be better to say that he released it. If he hadn't released it, if there had been any question of conscious invention, he couldn't have written the second act first. I don't personally find this in the least surprising, since I can't begin a novel until the ending comes to me. The ending arrives of its own accord, it arrives as a picture and not an abstract idea, it must be *seen* as a moment from life and, no matter how often I may revise what precedes it, I never depart from the original ending. I state this because it is relevant, not in an attempt to compare myself with Priestley. The fact is that Act Two, set in 1937, couldn't have been written unless Acts One and Three, set in 1919, had been already written. The terrible poignancy of Act Two, the shattering revelation of what Time has done to the Conways, depends entirely upon having been there with them on Kay's twenty-first birthday party in 1919. Priestley had to be there, a spectator at the party. A creative writer doesn't devise events and work consciously back: the result would be a made-up jigsaw puzzle, not an organic whole.

Time, it appears at first sight, is not the Time of Ouspensky and Dunne. It is Time the ever-rolling stream, Time the voyager of our hopes and dreams. It turns Hazel, the golden young creature, into a pale shadow of her husband, it turns Madge, the burning idealist, into a bitter spinster schoolmarm, it turns Robin, the dashing young RAF officer, into a boozy failure, it turns the pretty and scatterbrained Jean, whom he marries, into a drab and whining fool, it turns Kay, the emerging writer, into a cynical journalist entangled joylessly with a married man, it turns the self-confident, loving and benign matriarch, Mrs Conway, into a silly old woman meddling her way through into bankruptcy. Gerald, whom Madge might have married, once had ideals and a generous heart. Time has dried him up, turned him into 'a dreary, conceited, middle-aged bachelor'. And Ernest, ambitious and pushing but human enough to be hurt, human enough to be in love, is now an arrogant and mean-spirited domestic tyrant, rejoicing in the downfall of the Conways, rejoicing in his domination of Hazel. Time has bloated him with power, robbed him of his humanity.

There are only two it has not touched. Carol, the youngest, is not changed. She was innocence, she was love, she was happiness, spontaneous and unfeigned, she was Perdita, she was Cordelia, she was Miranda:

Hazel: Oh, Mother – I'd forgotten about Carol – it's sixteen years ago.
Alan: Seventeen.
Hazel (*in melancholy wonder*): Why, my Margaret's nearly as big as she was. Doesn't that seem strange, Kay?
Kay: I'd nearly forgotten about Carol too.
Mrs C (*with some emotion*): Don't think I had – because I was so stupid about that grave. I'm not one of those people who remember graves, it's human beings I remember. Only the other day, when I was sitting upstairs, I heard Carol shouting 'Mo-ther, mo-ther' – you know how she used to do. And then I began thinking about her, my poor darling, and how she came in that awful day, her face quite greyish, and said, 'Mother, I've the most sickening pain,' and then it was too late when they operated –

82

Hazel: Yes, Mother, we remember.

Ernest (*harsh and astonishing*): I'll tell you what you don't remember – and what some of you never even knew. She was the best of the lot – that one – little Carol – worth all the rest of you put together.

Hazel (*a shocked wife*): Ernest!

Ernest: Yes, and I'm counting you in. You were the one I wanted – that's all right, I got the one I wanted – but it didn't take me two hours to see that little Carol was the best of the lot. (*Adds gloomily*) Didn't surprise me when she went off like that. Out! Finish! Too good to last.

Mrs C (*now near to tears*): Ernest is quite right. She was the best of you all. My darling baby, I haven't forgotten you, I haven't forgotten you. (*Rising*) Oh, why isn't Robin here? (*Begins weeping, also moves away*) Go on, Gerald, explaining to them. I shan't be long. Don't move. (*Goes out in tears*)

And Alan is not touched by Time. Alan is the only one of the Conways left living at home, gentle, shabby, serene, with a routine job at the Town Hall. Alone at the family conference – ironically enough, on Kay's fortieth birthday – he is content, he accepts, nothing that he has had has been spoiled. The others, one way or another, are in prison, raging at their chains.

Gerald, with a certain dreary relish, explains in detail to Mrs Conway how hopeless her financial position is. Hazel suggests that Ernest lend her two or three thousand pounds, which will solve all her problems. Ernest gloatingly refuses. He tells them that when he first got into this house he thought he'd 'got somewhere'. But they were so 'high and mighty' that he resolved that one day he'd have his revenge. He'd humiliate them as they humiliated him.

The quarrel boils up to a climax when Mrs Conway slaps Ernest's face and he and Hazel leave the house. When they've gone the recriminations begin, they all turn on each other:

Madge (*with deadly deliberation*): I know how I'd have despised myself if I'd turned out to be a bad mother.

Mrs C (*angrily, rising*): So that's what you call me? (*Pauses, then with more vehemence and emotion*) Just because you never think of anybody but yourselves. All selfish – selfish. Because everything hasn't happened as you wanted it, turn on me – all my fault. You never really think

about me. Don't try to see things for a moment from my point
of view. When you were children, I was so proud of you all, so
confident that you would grow up to be wonderful creatures. I
used to see myself at the age I am now, surrounded by you and
your own children, so proud of you, so happy with you all, this
house happier and gayer even than it was in the best of the old days.
And now my life's gone by, and what's happened? You're a resent-
ful soured schoolmistress, middle-aged before your time. Hazel –
the loveliest child there ever was – married to a vulgar little bully,
and terrified of him. Kay here – gone away to lead her own life,
and very bitter and secretive about it, as if she'd failed. Carol – the
happiest and kindest of you all – dead before she's twenty. Robin
– I know, my dear, I'm not blaming you now, but I must speak
the truth for once – with a wife he can't love and no sort of position
or comfort or anything. And Alan – the eldest, the boy his father
adored, that he thought might do anything – what's he now? (*Alan
has come in now and is standing there quietly listening*) A miserable clerk
with no prospects, no ambition, no self-respect, a shabby little man
that nobody would look at twice. (*She sees him standing there now,
but in her worked-up fury does not care, and lashes out at him*) Yes, a
shabby clerk that nobody would look at twice.

Alan is unmoved, not because he does not care but because he can
see that his mother is a prisoner, and he is free. A free man has nothing
to rage about. Left alone with Kay, he tries to explain, tries to set
her free:

Alan: No, Time's only a kind of dream, Kay. If it wasn't, it would have
to destroy everything – the whole universe – and then remake it again
every tenth of a second. But Time doesn't destroy anything. It
merely moves us on – in this life – from one peep-hole to the next.
Kay: But the happy young Conways, who used to play charades here,
they've gone, and gone for ever.
Alan: No, they're real and existing, just as we two, here and now, are real
and existing. We're seeing another bit of the view – a bad bit, if
you like – but the whole landscape's still there.
Kay: But, Alan, we can't be anything but what we are *now*.
Alan: No ... it's hard to explain ... suddenly like this ... there's a book
I'll lend you – read it in the train. But the point is, now, at this
moment, or any moment, we're only a cross-section of our real

selves. What we *really* are is the whole stretch of ourselves, all our time, and when we come to the end of this life, all those selves, all our time, will be *us* – the real you, the real me. And then perhaps we'll find ourselves in another time, which is only another kind of dream.

I feel that in Priestley's place I would have cut the mention of the book, I wouldn't indeed have had Alan read a book about Time, I would have had him create the truth about Time for himself, from his deepest instincts. And that truth would be Sarah's in *Eden End* – 'There's a better place than this.' Sarah was not consciously talking about Time but she was creating the truth about Time from her deepest instincts and the truth is that there is another place, another time. But all this amounts to is spots on the sun. It is wrong and vulgar to grade works of art but of all Priestley's plays this is the most deeply satisfying. 'It cannot be too strongly emphasised,' Priestley says, 'that this play is not merely working a trick by reversing the last two acts, but that its whole point and quality are contained in the third act, when we know so much more about the characters than they know themselves ...'

He puts his finger on it. What sustains our interest in Act One and Two is a straightforward narrative interest, the pleasure is in having our curiosity aroused and then satisfied. But when we return to Kay's twenty-first birthday party the play enters a dimension of being – of being rather than feeling – not experienced with any other play. There is a sort of line, a line rather than a pattern, running through every work of art, like Hogarth's Line of Beauty. The line here is perfect: as simple and as obvious and as dazzlingly original as Nelson's battle plan at Trafalgar which, so the story runs, made his captains weep with sheer joy at its beauty. Technique by the wrong sort of writer is indeed regarded as a trick, a way of manipulating the subject matter. But in *Time and the Conways* they are one. If this is not a great play, I do not know what greatness is.

There followed from the autumn of 1937 a year into which few other writers could have crammed so much. He revised and helped to cast *People at Sea* which was being produced at the Bradford Civic Playhouse, he went to the USA on a four-week lecture tour, he wrote a series of articles for a Sunday paper, he wrote the novel *The Dooms-day Men* in three weeks, he began and nearly finished *Johnson Over Jordan*, he wrote *Music at Night* and *When We Are Married* – it wasn't merely a question of him using his time, but squeezing the last second out of each minute. Or rather as if he'd come to some arrangement with Time itself, had been given at least twice the normal ration. What he did in Arizona – where he spent the winter after the lecture tour – would have been a good year's work for any other professional writer. And in Arizona he had the idea for *Music at Night*.

This idea returned to him when, back in London, he was reminded of his promise in 1937 to contribute a new play to the Malvern Festival. He had always been a supporter of the Malvern Festival and was enthusiastic about the idea of six new plays instead of 'under-rehearsed specimens of our centuries of English drama performed in a very stuffy theatre'. In any case – another aspect of the puritan and the professional ethic – he had to honour his promise. And there was only a month to go before rehearsals began.

Fortunately, as he says in *Rain Upon Godshill*, the idea which he had in Arizona excited him:

> I would attempt to dramatise the mental adventures of a group of people listening to the first performance of a piece of music. It would be assumed that the music more or less controls their moods, but at the same time the progress throughout the play would be from the surface of the mind to deeper and deeper levels of consciousness ...

He had written plays within less than a month in the past, but the pressure then had been the pressure of creation and not a deadline imposed by others. The deadline may have shaken even Priestley's confidence. No matter how great his achievement, no matter how unblemished his record for delivery on time, there can come a moment for the professional writer when he feels that either he won't meet the deadline – which is the supreme professional sin for which he'll never forgive himself – or he'll deliver inferior work, which is even more unforgivable. To begin the play was easy:

> It did not take me long to assemble the characters and start the play going, but after that it was very hard work, and I had to do it against time, with one eye on the calendar. It had to be cast long before it was finished, and

1 Priestley's birthplace: 34
Mannheim Road, Bradford

2 Darley Street, the main
shopping street in Bradford
(c. 1891) with the exterior of
Kirkgate Market on the left

3 The Town Hall, Bradford, in 1903 : 'a noble building in the Italian Renaissance style'

4 A wool mill at Saltaire, near Bradford

5 Priestley's home (third from the left) at 5 Saltburn Place, 1904–14: 'This house, solidly built of stone, cost about £550 ... an unbelievable bargain.'

6 Lister Park, Bradford, in the 1920s but hardly changed from 1914, when Priestley wrote: 'A good place, a good time for the beginning of love'

7 The Cow and Calf Rocks on Ilkley Moor, within easy walking distance of Bradford

8 Machine-gun posts in the shell-holes at Passchendale Ridge, 1917

The Author
of
"The Good
Companions"
--With his
Good
Companions.

THE AUTHOR OF "THE GOOD COMPANIONS" AND "ANGEL PAVEMENT" AT HIS TYPEWRITER:
MR. J. B. PRIESTLEY—SNAPPED BY MRS. PRIESTLEY.

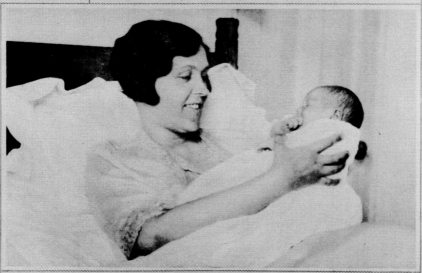

"GOOD COMPANIONS" OF THE AUTHOR OF "THE GOOD COMPANIONS": MRS. J. B. PRIESTLEY AND HER INFANT DAUGHTER.

Mr. J. B. Priestley is the distinguished author of "The Good Companions," the celebrated picaresque novel which enjoyed such an enormous success, and is said to have brought its author in the sum of £16,000—less income tax! His latest book, "Angel Pavement," has just appeared; and he has also just become the father of a new little daughter. Our photographs show Mrs. Priestley with the infant Miss Priestley, and Mr. Priestley with his typewriter—actually at work on the manuscript of his latest book. Mrs. Priestley took the photograph herself, at their home at Kingswear, Devonshire.

PHOTOGRAPH OF MRS. PRIESTLEY BY P. AND A.P.

10 The original cast of *The Good Companions*, His Majesty's Theatre, 1931

11 Musical version of *The Good Companions*, starring Judi Dench and John Mills (*centre*) and Christopher Gable (*left*), 1974

12 Flora Robson (*seated right*) in *Dangerous Corner*, 1932

13 At G. B. Shaw's garden party at Malvern, August 1932 (*left to right*) Jane
Priestley (his second wife), Sir Edward Elgar, Mrs Claude Beddington and J. B.
Priestley

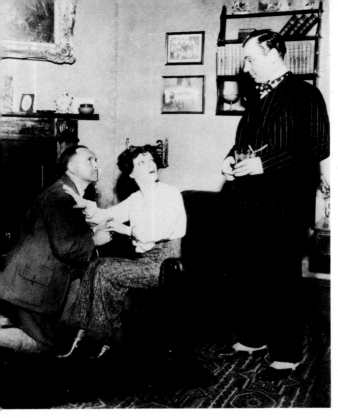

14 It was in the part of Charles Appelby that Ralph Richardson (*right*) first made an impression on Basil Dean, who was later to produce him in *Johnson Over Jordan*. *Eden End* with Beatrix Lehman, Duchess Theatre, 1934

15 Priestley and his wife Jane reading with their children in the drawing room of Billingham Manor, 1933

though the cast, with a few exceptions, was reasonably good, I could not help feeling uncomfortable. I fairly sweated at the piece, and once weakly telephoned Ayliff that it could not be done in time. He was so alarmed, for now the Festival had been announced, that I promised to have another try, and after a day or two's rest I grappled with the tortuous thing again. It was like wrestling eight hours a day with a gigantic eel ...

Music at Night was miraculously finished. The strain – strain even for Priestley – was lifted. Once more, against all the odds, the professional had delivered. A lesser man – which when one comes to think of it, means any other living writer – would have gone away for a long holiday. But another idea had descended upon Priestley:

No sooner had I seen a rehearsal or two of *Music at Night* than I was writing, very happily and at a furious speed, a farcical comedy that came finally to be called *When We Are Married*. My wife had given me the germ of the idea when we were crossing from America, for she had found in the ship's library an oldish volume of French short stories, and one of these stories had amused her by describing how a couple who were celebrating the anniversary of their wedding suddenly discovered they had never been married at all. I had long wanted to write a funny play about the Yorkshire d known as a boy, thirty years ago; so I took three couples instead ne, made it their silver wedding celebration, sketched in one or two s of genuine comedy (notably, that between Councillor Albert Parker is rebellious little wife in Act Three, which is, in my opinion, good ic comedy), and then, trying to remember every droll thing about d Yorkshire, I let it rip. Often I laughed while I was writing, not e I thought I was being very witty, but because memories of favourite of that period, such as 'flabbergasted', came back to me, and it was n introducing them all into the text. Actually, behind its farcical he little piece is not a bad sly sketch of provincial manners and atti- nd I was disappointed that some critics – one or two of them North men too – failed to remark its undercurrent of genuine sharp satire, ld not help wondering, somewhat wistfully, what they would have is had been an Irish – or even an American – play instead of a Yorkshire one.

We Are Married (first called *Wedding Group*) was produced Martin's in October 1938 and was an enormous success from I hesitate to use the word 'beloved' about a play, but this is one of the few for which no other word fits. It went well from the very start. 'Rehearsals went swimmingly,' Basil Dean said in his autobiography.

Priestley seemed thoroughly to enjoy his own characters, much as I imagine Dickens must have done. And why not? They were real people to him, not a set of imagined characters displayed for the audience's inspection ... We opened at the Opera House, Manchester, on September 19th, and stayed a week, playing to packed houses, the laughter growing louder at each performance. It seemed that Jack's was the voice the people wanted to hear at this time (the Munich Crisis): confident and strong, native humours untarnished by any alien influence. The Manchester critics fairly let themselves go, each one picking out a character for his special appreciation, yes even among the lesser roles ... A senior critic neatly summed up the whole affair: 'This is not only a "night out" for Mr Priestley, the serious dramatist, but for all of us who want to forget Europe for an hour or two ...'

London confirmed Manchester's verdict, the critics and the audiences acclaiming it with delight. After the opening there was a disaster when Frank Pettingell, who played the drunken phographer, was involved in a road accident. Priestley had red work on *Johnson Over Jordan* when he heard the news:

I agreed to go on and play the part myself until a real actor, v have to learn the lines and be properly rehearsed, could take less than twenty-four hours' notice, and discovered to my had not even a copy of the play in the house. The part, v of a drunken droll Yorkshire photographer, did not call f it was a mixture of fruity character-acting and sheer clo tained scores and scores of lines that had to be very ne amount of comic business, and in the Third Act, whe were in the action were being unravelled, it demar sure work with the rest of the company ... I did no of myself for a few nights, but I was very anxious play and the work of the professionals.

Early in 1939 *Johnson Over Jordan* went int Richardson as Johnson and Basil Dean once though the cast, with a few exceptions, was reasonably good, I could not help feeling uncomfortable. I fairly sweated at the piece, and once weakly telephoned Ayliff that it could not be done in time. He was so alarmed, for now the Festival had been announced, that I promised to have another try, and after a day or two's rest I grappled with the tortuous thing again. It was like wrestling eight hours a day with a gigantic eel . . .

Music at Night was miraculously finished. The strain – strain even for Priestley – was lifted. Once more, against all the odds, the professional had delivered. A lesser man – which when one comes to think of it, means any other living writer – would have gone away for a long holiday. But another idea had descended upon Priestley:

No sooner had I seen a rehearsal or two of *Music at Night* than I was writing, very happily and at a furious speed, a farcical comedy that came finally to be called *When We Are Married*. My wife had given me the germ of the idea when we were crossing from America, for she had found in the ship's library an oldish volume of French short stories, and one of these stories had amused her by describing how a couple who were celebrating the anniversary of their wedding suddenly discovered they had never been married at all. I had long wanted to write a funny play about the Yorkshire I had known as a boy, thirty years ago; so I took three couples instead of one, made it their silver wedding celebration, sketched in one or two scenes of genuine comedy (notably, that between Councillor Albert Parker and his rebellious little wife in Act Three, which is, in my opinion, good sardonic comedy), and then, trying to remember every droll thing about that old Yorkshire, I let it rip. Often I laughed while I was writing, not because I thought I was being very witty, but because memories of favourite words of that period, such as 'flabbergasted', came back to me, and it was such fun introducing them all into the text. Actually, behind its farcical bustle, the little piece is not a bad sly sketch of provincial manners and attitudes. And I was disappointed that some critics – one or two of them North Countrymen too – failed to remark its undercurrent of genuine sharp satire, and I could not help wondering, somewhat wistfully, what they would have said if this had been an Irish – or even an American – play instead of a homely Yorkshire one.

When We Are Married (first called *Wedding Group*) was produced at the St Martin's in October 1938 and was an enormous success from the start. I hesitate to use the word 'beloved' about a play, but this is one of the few for which no other word fits. It went well from the very start. 'Rehearsals went swimmingly,' Basil Dean said in his autobiography.

Priestley seemed thoroughly to enjoy his own characters, much as I imagine Dickens must have done. And why not? They were real people to him, not a set of imagined characters displayed for the audience's inspection . . . We opened at the Opera House, Manchester, on September 19th, and stayed a week, playing to packed houses, the laughter growing louder at each performance. It seemed that Jack's was the voice the people wanted to hear at this time (the Munich Crisis): confident and strong, native humours untarnished by any alien influence. The Manchester critics fairly let themselves go, each one picking out a character for his special appreciation, yes even among the lesser roles . . . A senior critic neatly summed up the whole affair: 'This is not only a "night out" for Mr Priestley, the serious dramatist, but for all of us who want to forget Europe for an hour or two . . .'

London confirmed Manchester's verdict, the critics and the audiences acclaiming it with delight. After the opening there was a disaster when Frank Pettingell, who played the drunken photographer, was involved in a road accident. Priestley had resumed work on *Johnson Over Jordan* when he heard the news:

I agreed to go on and play the part myself until a real actor, who would have to learn the lines and be properly rehearsed, could take over. I had less than twenty-four hours' notice, and discovered to my horror that I had not even a copy of the play in the house. The part, which was that of a drunken droll Yorkshire photographer, did not call for any subtlety; it was a mixture of fruity character-acting and sheer clowning; but it contained scores and scores of lines that had to be very neatly timed, a certain amount of comic business, and in the Third Act, when such knots as there were in the action were being unravelled, it demanded some quick and sure work with the rest of the company . . . I did not mind making a fool of myself for a few nights, but I was very anxious not to spoil my own play and the work of the professionals.

Early in 1939 *Johnson Over Jordan* went into rehearsal with Ralph Richardson as Johnson and Basil Dean once again as producer. In

the dedication he calls the play 'this adventure of the theatre' and
that is exactly what it is. 'Here, for the first time,' he says in the Preface, 'I tried to make use of all the resources of the theatre, including
music and ballet . . .'

What he set out to do, what in fact he triumphantly accomplished,
was something which only he could have had the breadth of vision
and the enormous self-confidence even to contemplate. Up till now
he had worked within the confines of the commercially practicable.
That is to say, practicable in terms of production. His plays virtually
all had single sets, casts of a reasonable size, and did not depend upon
elaborate special effects. The rawest amateur dramatic society can
produce *Laburnum Grove* in the village hall. It won't be the same
– and that's an understatement – as the Albery production with
Arthur Lowe as George, but the play will be there, there will be,
however imperfectly realized, some of the magic. And a repertory
company can produce the same play, and make a profit. And again,
some of the magic will be still there.

The art of the producer in the theatre is much more than ensuring
the proper delivery of the speeches. It is, to render it down to essen-
tials, the orchestration of those words with movement and, perhaps
most important of all, with silence. Movement – within which is
included every kind of physical gesture and expression – is in fact
what makes a play. The movement isn't an illustration of the words.
It's co-existent with the words but at the same time independent of
the words. One step forward can say as much as a page of dialogue;
but if the dialogue hadn't preceded it, it would mean nothing.

Putting aside considerations such as lighting, all this means a complex and demanding act of sustained creation, even with a straight
play, a small cast, and a single set. Add music and ballet and the complexity further increases. For the music and ballet in *Johnson Over
Jordan* are not subsidiary to the words. The purpose of using them
is to do what words can't do. Then have a multiplicity of scenes,
each with different lighting, and a cast of twenty-three, eleven of
whom are the named characters and twelve of whom are supporting
characters and, for want of a better word, extras. The latter will,
whenever possible, double-up, but they are something very much
more than spear-carriers, crowd-players. Each one of them must be ·

regarded as being just as essential to the play as the principal characters, each move worked out. And when there are words the words
are not 'rhubarb rhubarb':

Voice from Loud-Speaker: All applicants with forms still not completed
must hurry now. Only a few minutes left.

> (*As Johnson tries to settle down with his form again
> two typical newspaper 'boys' come hurrying on, one
> at each side of the desk, and begin calling out in
> their usual style.*)

First Newspaper Boy: All abou' the big dee-saster.
Second Newspaper Boy: All abou' the 'orrible murder.
First Newspaper Boy: All abou' the Cri-sis.
Second Newspaper Boy: All abou' the fall o' Peking, Barcelona,
Madrid.
First Newspaper Boy: All abou' the end o' Rome, Vienna, Berlin,
Paris.
Second Newspaper Boy: All abou' the burning o' London.
First Newspaper Boy: All abou' the Great Plague.
Second Newspaper Boy: All abou' the end o' the world.

> (*Up to the last two or three cries, Johnson has resisted
> them, but now he comes forward, putting his hand
> in his pocket for coppers, feeling very anxious.*)

Johnson: Here, what's all this?
First Newspaper Boy: (*coolly*): All the winners.
Second Newspaper Boy (*hopefully*): Duke stung by wasp.
Johnson (*annoyed*): Go on. Clear out.

> (*They hurry out. Johnson returns to the desk and
> starts on the form again, but the music begins, and
> a solitary clerk-dancer appears and performs his
> antics just in front of where Johnson is sitting. John-
> son rises angrily.*)

Johnson (*shouting*): Oh – for God's sake – stop that. Get
out – and stay out.

> (*He takes a few menacing steps towards the clerk,
> who hurries out through one of the office doors. The
> light changes, the desk no longer being brilliantly
> illuminated, and, in a more normal light, Mr Clay-
> ton strides in through one of the small proscenium*

doors. He is at least twenty-five years younger than he was when we saw him in the hall of Johnson's house, and of course he is dressed like a prosperous City man of the pre-War period. He is extremely angry.)

From this short extract – the playing time would be no more than three minutes – may be gauged the complexity of the producer's task. Johnson's dialogue with the newspaper boys is straightforward enough, though his business with the form is far more difficult than would be supposed from the stage directions. He must be genuinely struggling with the form, he must engage our sympathy, he must interest us. *Business* is a convenient stage term, but there is really no business, only *acting*. When the newspaper boys exit, the music begins. It must be timed to the split second and the dancer takes up the beat. A split second out either way and the scene goes out of key. And the dancer must be more than a dancer, he must actually hear Johnson tell him to go away. The light changes; and if the timing is out by a split second the scene won't change. And Clayton, since we last saw him, has had to make up again and change his clothes. And his make-up hasn't been a simple matter of taking something off or putting something on.

All this is merely to indicate a few of the problems involved in the phrase 'all the resources of the theatre'. And one doesn't take into account the question of pace over and above the organization of detail. Detail can be worked out consciously with the front half of the mind; but the pace of a play can only be determined by instinct. Basil Dean, with whom Priestley had a long-standing and fruitful association in the theatre and the cinema, was one of the few producers capable of meeting the challenge:

When he handed me the script of *Johnson Over Jordan*, a modern morality, in which the outstanding events in a man's life flit through the middle years of temptation, thence to unsullied youth – a life history in reverse order as it were – I realized that it would afford some opportunities not only for the display of Ralph's gifts, but also give me a chance to resume my experiments in new production methods.

Purely fortuitously on a visit to his son at Cambridge, Dean was introduced to Benjamin Britten, then comparatively unknown, and asked him to compose the music for the play. The designer was Edward Craig, the son of Gordon Craig:

We were both sufficiently under the influence of his father's genius to rule out the possibility of any divergence in the broad sweep of our ideas. We decided upon a simple open setting: draperies of hessian canvas, of great height, hung in wide, sweeping curves from the grid on special tracks: in the background two cycloramas, one behind the other; the rear cyclorama made, painted and hung in accordance with Max Hasdit's technique; the one in front of fine blue silk, made to part in the middle – each to be lighted as though the other did not exist; hardly any scenery in the accepted sense, just a significant door or window to indicate locality, and a few pieces of furniture for similar purpose. Today a denuded stage is so commonplace as to arouse no comment, but I am writing of more than thirty years ago ...

New ground was being broken. Priestley and Dean were not only using all the resources of the theatre, but devising new resources, new techniques, taking the theatre forward, increasing its potentialities. The lighting was a new development: 'We literally painted over draperies with light', Dean records,

in sympathy with the mood of the events which Johnson was experiencing. With new techniques came new problems, which were all solved with a speed which now seems incredible.

The play was presented at the New Theatre on February 22nd, 1939, and received an ovation, which was repeated on the second and all subsequent nights.

It was a triumph of the highest order, it was Priestley's supreme moment in the theatre. It was Ralph Richardson's supreme moment, a moment which he and Priestley remember to this day.

Much of the excitement [Dean said] was due to the closing moments of the play when Johnson, carrying umbrella and brief-case, began his ascent into the unknown. Benjamin Britten's thrilling music, added to the blue immensity that I had contrived with my two cycloramas, never failed to bring down the house. On the first night, standing at the back of the pit, I found myself gulping down involuntary tears ...

For the end of *Johnson Over Jordan* is its beginning. It isn't about life after death, it is about a new life which Johnson with pain and difficulty chooses. Johnson isn't going to Hell or Heaven, Johnson isn't dead. Only his body has died. The body was real, but so is the Johnson who walks into the blue immensity. Johnson is there all of the time. The play is in fact part of a larger play which began with *I Have Been Here Before* and continued with *Time and the Conways*. It's not in any sense the final play in a trilogy. It stands by itself. And it continues, it is a prologue to Johnson's journey. I saw the Bradford Civic production, and am always grateful that I did. It was a magnificent production, but cannot be compared with the New Theatre production – how could it? But now as I write, I look back and remember going out of the theatre into the Bradford streets, taken out of myself, a citizen of eternity, strangely exultant and free; and I understand Dean's tears, I too saw Richardson begin his journey into the blue immensity.

The play ran for three weeks. Some of the critics acclaimed it for what it was, recognized instantly its power and grandeur, its enormous range, its masterly use of new techniques. They could see what Basil Dean saw, they too became citizens of eternity, they gave themselves to the play. Others, the pygmies, had nothing to give, saw the play as Priestley's first failure, alluded to German Expressionism in terms which made it clear that they understood nothing about it. German Expressionism essentially was about abstractions, *Johnson Over Jordan* about individual human beings. But the play, because of the financial structure of the company producing it, seems to have been doomed from the start. In their praiseworthy enthusiasm to bring the drama to the people, Priestley and his associates had put themselves into an impossible position. They could either lose or break even; they couldn't make a profit. And this is another Priestley paradox. There was, there still is in some quarters, an image of him as the hard-headed Yorkshireman coolly calculating what the public likes, and translating that calculation into hard cash. The truth is the exact opposite: not only does he not care about money, but it would have been better for him if he had cared rather more. It goes without saying that, to this day, he has received no thanks for what he did for the British theatre without thought of personal profit.

Johnson Over Jordan marked the end of an era. It did not, of course, mark the end of his career as a dramatist, although in his understandable bitterness at fate he did consider making it his last play. The bitterness did not last long. There were new ideas clamouring to be expressed and a new phase beginning in his life and the life of the nation.

5

The Compassionate Eye

Before that new phase can be examined it is necessary to consider another aspect of his work. I use the term social criticism for want of a better one and I take into account what he himself has said:

> Unlike many contemporary writers, I have always believed that novels (and plays) should be entertaining. But that does not mean – as some silly reviewers, especially in America, seem to think – that my novels are entertainment and nothing else. There is always a great deal of social criticism in them, together with much symbolism, both in the action and the characters ...

This is not of course to say that he is committed (or, to use the trendier term, *engagé*), that his novels and plays are the means to a political end. He is first and foremost an artist, his purpose is creative rather than didactic. But novels and plays deal with individual characters not in isolation but in society. There is a germ of truth in Marx's law of economic determinism. As characters we aren't wholly shaped by our economic environment, but the kind of society we live in – particularly during our formative years – is as important as our genes. And literature, unlike music, is not a pure art. It is essentially moral. The art of the writer is much more than self-expression. To reveal the truth about his society, no less than about his characters, is a condition of his art. And to reveal the truth is to criticize, which is the first step towards working for a better society. Not to condemn what is bad about our society is equivalent to accepting the bad as good. To regard art as being wholly a form of self-expression is to make of it merely a high-grade masturbation. The writer who isn't

95

passionately concerned in building a more just society is like an ss man conducting the prisoners' orchestra in a concentration camp.

Social criticism isn't, however, a literary form as the novel is. At least, it isn't with lesser writers. But Priestley's huge energy made a new form, which still lacks a proper term to describe it. The books – *English Journey*, *Midnight on the Desert*, *Rain upon Godshill* – which I am about to consider, are travel and autobiography in the librarian's sense. Or, to put it in another way, they're Priestley talking to us in his own person. They are each works of art: the Muse has descended upon each one. They are not relaxations from serious work, books into which are crammed odds and ends which wouldn't fit anywhere else. The subject of *English Journey* is the autumn of 1933, the subject of *Midnight on the Desert* and *Rain upon Godshill* the course of his life and thoughts from the time of his first winter in Arizona to the time of the production of *Johnson Over Jordan*. Over and above this they record Priestley's ceaseless search for the truth. They are indeed entertaining, they have, especially in the two autobiographical volumes, the quality of good conversation. But they are conversations, not monologues.

I approached *English Journey* again, after an interval of over thirty years, with even more trepidation than I had approached *Angel Pavement*. I half-expected it to have dated, to be old journalism between hard covers. But it read as freshly as at the first reading. Priestley began his journey, in the autumn of 1933, from Southampton, travelling to Bristol and Swindon, the Cotswolds, Coventry, Birmingham and the Black Country, Leicester and Nottingham, the West Riding, the Potteries, Lancashire, the Tyne, East Durham and the Tees, Lincoln and Norfolk, and from there back to Highgate Village.

As will be seen, he didn't attempt to be comprehensive, to cover every corner of every county. His intention was to show the enormous variety of England and in this he succeeded. Not every writer can convey the spirit of place but this has been one of his special gifts from the very beginning. The book, of course, has serious points to make, it is a savage indictment of the England of 1933. He does not hope for any easy solutions, particularly not for political solutions:

People are beginning to believe that government is a mysterious process with which they have no real concern. This is the soil in which autocracies flourish and liberty dies. Alongside that apathetic majority there will soon be a minority that is tired of seeing nothing vital happen and that will adopt any cause that promises decisive action.

Above all it is the expression of his deep love for his native country:

Never once have I arrived in a foreign country and cried, 'This is the place for me.' I would rather spend a holiday in Tuscany than in the Black Country, but if I were compelled to choose between living in West Bromwich or Florence, I should make straight for West Bromwich ... I am probably bursting with blatant patriotism ... And my patriotism, I assured myself, does begin at home. There is a lot of pride in it ... Why, this little country of ours has known so many great men and great ideas that one's mind is dazzled by its riches. We stagger beneath our inheritance ... We have led the world, many a time before today ... We can lead it again. We headed the procession when it took what we see now to be the wrong turning, down into the dark bog of greedy industrialism, where money and machines are of more importance than men and women. It is for us to find the way out again, into the sunlight. We may have to risk a great deal, perhaps our very existence. But rather than live on meanly and savagely, I concluded, it would be better to perish as the last of the civilized peoples ...

However, it has another dimension. Once again there is the pleasure of the journey, the poetry of departure. Nothing is seen in the abstract, we are with Priestley every inch of the way. We see through his eyes, we hear with his ears, but we're not looking inside but outside. Every detail is filled in, nothing is missed out; but there is much more to the book than description. The agreeable Dickensian sub-title: 'A rambling but truthful account of what one man saw and heard and felt and thought during a journey through England', is entirely accurate except that it is the absolute opposite of rambling, being a completely integrated whole, a sustained and seamless narrative rather than a collection of loosely connected set pieces.

The feelings and the thoughts stem naturally from what Priestley sees and hears. There isn't any division between abstract and concrete. The thoughts arise out of the descriptions as if somehow they were part of the object described, as solid as the object. The thoughts are metaphors, the metaphors are thoughts, the flow is uninterrupted from sentence to sentence, between paragraph and paragraph, between chapter and chapter. There is never a hint of the contrived, the metaphors aren't stuck on like labels but are part of the flow of the narrative:

After the familiar muddle of West London, the Great West Road looked very odd. Being new, it did not look English. We might have suddenly rolled into California. Or, for that matter, into one of the main avenues of the old exhibitions, like the Franco-British Exhibition of my boyhood. It was the line of new factories on each side that suggested the exhibition, for years of the West Riding have fixed for ever my idea of what a proper factory looks like; a grim blackened rectangle with a tall chimney at one corner. These decorative little buildings, all glass and concrete and chromium plate, seem to my barbaric mind to be merely playing at being factories ...

The strength of this description is precisely that it's relaxed, the tone of voice is easy, conversational, the rhythms are the rhythms of speech. The thought – and it really is a metaphor – that the new factories, the light industry factories, don't look like proper factories at all, strikes one as being very sensible, precisely what one has always thought – but somehow or other has never put into words. Most of the statement is, however, beneath the surface. What Priestley is also commenting upon is the decline of the industrial North, the home of heavy industry. Priestley's prose – and it's one of the main reasons for his enormous productivity, it's the area big enough to accommodate the three-ring circus – contains this without strain and foreshadows future stages of the journey without portentousness.

That is only one side of the book. It isn't only about places, it's about people. Indeed, Priestley would say that one can't write about a place without writing about its people. Indeed, the book begins with a full-length portrait of a man with whom Priestley strikes up acquaintance in the charabanc to Southampton:

He was a thinnish fellow, somewhere in his forties, and he had a sharp nose, a neat moustache, rimless eyeglasses, and one of those enormous foreheads, roomy enough for an Einstein, that so often do not seem to mean anything. The rimless eyeglasses gave him that very keen look which also often means nothing; and at first he suggested those men who are drawn or photographed for advertisements of American Insurance companies. He looked capable of rationalizing huge muddled industries. It was a face with which you could have rescued the cotton trade in Lancashire. But, as so often happens, the man behind the face was quite different. He was neither strong nor silent, but a very ordinary human being, one of us, uncertain, weakish, garrulous, always vaguely hoping that a miracle would be worked for him. Like so many men in business, he was at heart a pure romantic ...

He tells Priestley about his dreams of making a fortune and, without knowing it, reveals to him his dismal failure as a businessman. But dismal is the wrong word. He is happy now to dream of riches through a patented pipe. He shows it to Priestley:

'Every time you've had a smoke, you change one of the pieces – they give you spares – and so it's always nice and clean and cool. Clever, isn't it?'

I admitted that it was ingenious. Actually, it looked and smelt horrible and dirty and hot; a loathsome little pipe ...

We do not see him again, he is not referred to again, he is not an essential part of the theme of the book, he doesn't symbolize anything. It could be argued that to describe him at any length is a piece of pure self-indulgence, Priestley showing off his power as a novelist. It might also be argued that the space taken up in his characterization would be better spent in describing the places the charabanc passes through. Yet if he were removed the book would be the poorer for it. He represents the assurance that the journey is a real journey and not merely a convenient framework for a book, that what is written about is what excited the interest of Priestley at the time. The book had not to have any predetermined pattern imposed upon it: it was not a topographical book written to order but a record of Priestley's spontaneous thoughts and reactions.

It would have been easy – and no doubt enormously profitable – for Priestley to have written a kind of non-fiction *Good Companions* with himself as the Good Companion. He could, as it were, have made his journey an escape and a holiday: there would have been a case for doing so. The book is of course supremely readable, it is far from being unrelievedly sombre. Yet it is a far more powerful condemnation of the England of the Thirties than is a book like *Love on the Dole*. There is one passage which stays especially in my mind:

> My second day there [in Birmingham] was a Sunday, and in foul weather ... I lunched in one of the smaller towns with a man in the metal trade ... There had been a sudden flurry of business in the metal trade, and my friend was going back to his office and warehouse in West Bromwich after lunch. I went with him ... My friend's warehouse was in – shall we say? – 'Rusty Lane', West Bromwich. He keeps sheets of steel there, and no doubt any place is good enough to keep sheets of steel in; but I do not think I could let even a sheet of steel stay long in Rusty Lane. I have never seen such a picture of grimy desolation as that street offered me. If you put it, brick for brick, into a novel, people would not accept it, would condemn you as a caricaturist and talk about Dickens. The whole neighbourhood is mean and squalid, but this particular street seemed the worst of all. It would not matter very much – though it would matter – if only metal were kept there; but it happens that people live there, children are born there and grow up there. I saw some of them. I was being shown one of the warehouses, where steel plates were stacked in the chill gloom, and we heard a bang and rattle on the roof. The boys, it seems, were throwing stones again. They were always throwing stones on that roof. We went out to find them, but only found three frightened little girls, who looked at us with round eyes in wet smudgy faces. No, they hadn't done it, the boys had done it, and the boys had just run away. Where they could run to, I cannot imagine. They need not have run away from me, because I could not blame them if they threw stones and stones and smashed every pane of glass for miles. Nobody can blame them if they grow up to smash everything that can be smashed ...

What stays in my mind is the three frightened little girls. I can see their round eyes and my tears begin to flow despite myself. And what Marx said about religion comes back to me: *Heart of the heartless world, hope of hopeless conditions* ... And that is what literature should be, that is what Priestley makes it in *English Journey*. I see no sign of a heart so compassionate among English writers today.

I have termed *Midnight on the Desert* and *Rain upon Godshill* autobiographical, and it's true that they cover the period in Priestley's life from the production of *Time and the Conways* in New York to the production of *Johnson Over Jordan* in London. But they are not about Priestley at all. They are about Priestley the writer, about his work and about his ideas. There is no picture of the private person, and only the briefest glimpse of his wife and children. There is here another Priestley paradox. He is possibly the best-known of twentieth-century writers, instantly recognizable and instantly recognized all over the world. There is no other writer whose face and whose personality is so firmly fixed in the public mind. There is something almost frightening about the sheer force and strength of his personality. He reminds me of no one but himself and there is no one else who reminds one of him. There is about him no effort to impress, no swirling round his shoulders of the purple cloak of the great writer. He is, as the saying goes, as easy as an old shoe, but the enormous force is there, quiet, apparently still. I remember a disc at the piston-ring factory where I worked briefly in my youth. It was some kind of grindstone and, so I was told, revolved at a fantastic speed. When I looked at it it seemed absolutely still but for the faintest of vibrations and the faintest of whines at the top of the register of the ear. After a minute one knew that the stillness was not stillness but speed, and the speed was energy. This is as near as I can get to summing up the quality of Priestley's *persona*. He himself isn't frightening, being essentially gentle and amiable and hospitable, but that tremendous energy is frightening, it has about it the terrible stillness of that disc at the factory.

The private person is not there in *Midnight on the Desert* and *Rain upon Godshill*. One isn't speaking of shocking revelations, one neither expects nor wants startling confessions. It is right and always has been right that Priestley should keep his private life private; I myself make absolutely no revelations about my private life. But the man revealed in *Midnight on the Desert* and *Rain upon Godshill* is Priestley the writer. A lesser man – or, one should say, a lesser writer – would have published the two books in notebook or diary form. Priestley made them into properly shaped books. They are in consequence about the ideas they contain. Again, it's as if the ideas had always been there and he had discovered them, rather than as if he had had the ideas. He looked outside himself rather than inside, and that is why they retain their value today.

What *Rain upon Godshill* does record is his continuing concern for the state of England, which was then sleep-walking into war. Nothing had changed since he wrote *English Journey*:

The problems seemed to be there still, only now with a deeper despair all round them. We were still being told to be proud of all those good things here that we did not create ourselves but that were left to us by our grandfathers ... But what creative effort were we making now? Where was our planning? Where was the noble national idea? We were always being told by those sections of the Press determined to be popular at all costs and to stop the people from thinking for themselves, how much better off we were than the people of other nations. And so we might well be, with more home comforts and fewer secret police, but what was the great creative idea that was inspiring us? ... Even the Nazis could believe they were purifying and strengthening the race, removing from their Reich the disabilities imposed upon it by the Treaty of Versailles, and building up a strong and self-reliant Germany. Even the Fascists could believe they were transforming Italy, which they saw once as a country indolently living on its past, into a formidable great power, boldly planning for the future. I could not agree with these ideas, but I could see that they could act as a kind of yeast, leavening the public mind. In Russia the young communists could believe they were creating a new civilization, in which for the first time in history the workers would reap the full harvest of their labour and the people would toil no longer for a privileged few. But where was our creative idea, what banner had we raised?

Shaped by his early upbringing, by his father's generous idealism and by his own robust courage, he still hoped for a better England, a new kind of society.

The English instinct has always been to treat economics and politics as a mere part of a man's life, and to consider a man's economic position and political opinions as less important than his general character and not to be confused with it ... You may declare that this attitude of mind belongs to yesterday, and that the realities of today can and will ignore it. But what about tomorrow? Here, in this temper of mind, it may be that there is a bridge that will take us from yesterday to tomorrow, from the end of one system of real communal life to the beginning of another and better one, safely across the iron and sterile gulfs of an enforced economy that has neither true politics nor community. In short, I believe the English to have qualities that would make it possible for the new society, which will

not be Communism or Fascism or capitalist democracy, to make a beginning here ...

He was, of course, well aware that unless there were profound
changes this new society could not be born. He had no illusions about
the England of 1939. There was nothing here for the comfort of the
middle classes, the middle classes who, as he had pointed out, bought
his books and tickets for his plays. He was not considering his best
interests, he was not considering what his public liked to hear. But
he was not, had never been, anxious to please the public. He set out
to entertain in the first place; there's no point in having an urgent
message if one's so boring that no one will listen. This chapter is
first-rate polemics – angry, biting, hard-hitting, complacency-dis-
pelling, burningly sincere. But it is more than entertainment. It
would indeed have been easy for him not to care, to retreat not to
his ivory tower but to his magnificent workroom at Godshill:

It has five big windows in a row; the three in the centre, about four
feet square, wind up and down like the windows in a motor-car; and then
at each end is an equally large curved one; so that the general effect, as
everybody notices, is of the bridge of a ship. (And don't forget it is on
the roof.) Once up here, I feel that the family ship happens to be at anchor
in the middle of the Isle of Wight, but that at any moment I can give the
signal and off we shall go. In between spells of work at the table, I can
pace up and down, and there is so much light and air that I don't feel as
one does in a study tucked away at the back of the ground floor, that I
am a prisoner of my work. I can see more up here, with the immensely
wide view sweeping across a quarter of the island, than if I stopped working
and went down into the garden ...

He could have stayed in the workroom, written about his work past
and future, he could have given his readers magic, he could with
a clear conscience have given them escape. He could at least have
promised salvation through the Labour Party. But he saw no real
hope in the Labour Party as it then was. 'My own objection to it
is that I distrust its trade union basis. Not that I dislike trade unions
in themselves, but I do not think they make a good foundation for
a national political party. To begin with, the system is not conspicu-
ously democratic ...' Prophetically, he went on to say: 'It does not
follow that because there are a great many railwaymen and transport

workers they will have a real national outlook, not coloured by any prejudices arising from class or occupation ... If we ever do build Jerusalem in England's green and pleasant land, it certainly will not be done under trade union rules ...'

In short, he attacked in all directions. He was his own man, the servant only of the truth as he saw it. And, prophetically again, he saw the dangers of what later he was to call Admass. 'You see a new kind of urban life now in the natty suburbs of the provincial cities and near all the main roads leading out of London. In theory and on paper it looks a pretty good life ...' He pointed out that a great many of the young couples who lived this sort of life were 'nearly as far removed from the main stream of civic life as those melancholy souls who exist perpetually in hotels. There is something thin, brittle, mechanical about their life. It lacks richness, human variety, sap and juice ...' He was not only foreseeing Admass but the deserts created by post-war redevelopment, the high-rise blocks which drove young women to suicide, the new city centres which ripped the heart out of the cities, the local government reorganization which deliberately destroyed the spirit of place, the monstrous alliance of private rapacity and bureaucratic stupidity which replaced the old slums with something infinitely worse, infinitely more destructive to the human spirit.

War broke out before *Rain upon Godshill* was published. It was reprinted immediately. Priestley, as always, had been right to say what he wanted to say and not what it might be assumed the people wanted to hear. Change was on the way. It would not be easy. But what it meant was this: there would be a new spirit, the language would be used in a different way. What Priestley said, in the chapter of *Rain upon Godshill* I've quoted from, didn't of course exactly fit what the people of England thought and felt. But what he essentially said – that we must rid ourselves of illusions, that we must depend upon each other, sustain each other, work as individuals for a common purpose – was what the nation was moving towards. Priestley had found some of the words. The nation from now on was only going to listen to those who spoke the truth. The nation had heard enough lies.

6

War and Commitment

To say that Britain – or rather the British Government – sleepwalked into war in 1939 is to libel sleepwalkers. For sleepwalkers traditionally never take a wrong step, bear a charmed life. The Government of the phoney war period never took the right step. Young though I was at the time, even I could understand that those who directed the nation literally didn't know what they were doing. Lunatics would have been preferable because occasionally by pure chance lunatics might have done the right thing. The fact that the French Government – which apparently believed that the Germans would never be so ungentlemanly as to bypass the Maginot Line – was equally incapable was no consolation. It wasn't that the nation was defeatist, and furthermore, it was clear even to the meanest intelligence what would happen to us if the Germans invaded. It was simply that there wasn't even the most elementary kind of leadership.

Churchill changed all that. He was a great leader, a statement hard to accept for some, partly because of the cloyingly adulatory terms in which it has been expressed by so many vulgar hacks, partly because his mistakes were so numerous and so huge, and partly because he was, undeniably, a monster, and the majority of those who pass historical judgements are liberal humanists who honestly believe that a war can be won with clean hands. However, Churchill was more often right than wrong, the majority of people are not liberal humanists and if Churchill was a monster he was an English monster, *our* kind of monster. He wasn't St George, he was our dragon, the English dragon who was going to kill the German dragon. It takes a dragon to kill a dragon.

The Second World War was a people's war. That's another simple truth which it's difficult to state now without self-consciousness. England didn't become classless overnight. But there was a new spirit, based on the fact that this was a war in which the civilian population was as much involved as the Armed Forces. There were no longer two Englands – Blighty and the Front, the safe civilian world and the hellish military world. The blitz at one stroke abolished the distinction between soldier and civilian. It was possible then to see in the future a new society of the kind that Priestley outlined in *Rain upon Godshill*. A new society, a *civitas Dei*, was no longer a naïve conception, it was outside party politics, it wasn't the creation of the wartime propaganda machine. It was based upon sharing, on a common purpose, on living for something outside oneself. But most of all it was based upon common suffering.

In *The Last Enemy*, Richard Hillary expressed it for us all. Richard Hillary was an exceptionally handsome and talented young man, the son of a well-to-do middle-class family, whose whole life at school, at university, and in the RAF as a fighter pilot had been a series of triumphs. Everything had come easily to Hillary, he was the golden boy and charming with it; he was not precisely a snob, not over-arrogant in a vulgar way, but he was well aware that he wasn't as other men, that he was one of the inheritors of the earth. He was shot down in combat, his face was terribly burned and then re-assembled by the skill of the surgeon, Archibald McIndoe. Perhaps no one but McIndoe could have given him any kind of face; ; but what he had now was a ravaged mask, the face of war. During the blitz in London one night he helped to clear the wreckage away from the bedroom of a bombed house. The woman who had been sleeping with her child in the bedroom was alive and conscious, but the child was dead.

I was at the head of the bed, and looking down into that tired, blood-streaked, work-worn face I had a sense of complete unreality. I took the brandy flask from my hip pocket and held it to her lips. Most of it ran down her chin, but a little flowed between those clenched teeth. She opened her eyes and reached out her arms instinctively for the child. Then she started to weep. Quite soundlessly, and with no sobbing, the tears were running down her cheeks when she lifted her eyes to mine. 'Thank you, sir,' she said, and took my hand in hers. And then, looking at me again, she said after a pause, 'I see they got you too.'

Hillary was still proud, still one of the inheritors of the earth, still different, but her words penetrated to his heart, and he understood. He and the old woman were of the same community, the community of suffering: *I see they got you too*. The passage cannot be read without tears even now.

Hillary went back on active service – though he need not have done – and died in combat. Thinking of him now, one feels a sense of sorrow but not of waste. It was that kind of war. It would have been infinitely better had it never happened; but, since it did happen, it is necessary to consider what kind of war it was. It was unique in being a People's War; it was also unique in being the first major war in which the leader told at least some of the truth to the people, treated them as adults. For Churchill offered the British people blood, sweat, and tears. And in so doing he paid them the compliment of treating them as adults. To have promised them easy victories and a golden tomorrow would have been to treat them like children.

I am not trying here to glamorize war or attempting in any way to minimize the suffering caused by it. And those who suffered in it, at the moment of their suffering, would not have formulated any of these noble thoughts. But this doesn't alter the fact that the Second World War was a war in which it was right to serve. It was a war in which the choice was nakedly between good and evil. Looking back at it, in *Margin Released*, Priestley summed up its special atmosphere:

The bright eyes of danger have never fascinated me. If I am not quite a coward, I am much closer to being one than I am to being any sort of hero. Yet I can honestly declare that on the whole I enjoyed that time ... Even later, during the buzz-bomb time, when I appeared to be fire watching every night in Albany, where I lived, and had to make do with about two hours' sleep ... I liked life in a West End that suddenly seemed to be empty. We were all an improvement on our unendangered selves. No longer suspicious of gaiety we almost sparkled. What more than half the English fear and detest is not threatened disaster, material insecurity, sacrifice or danger, but boredom ... There is of course among us, too widely reflected in our legislation, a minority of life-haters, enemies of everything sensuous and generous, adventurous and creative. In 1940 to 1941, for once, the rest of us escaped from their influence, felt free, companionable, even – except where waiting for the explosion – lighthearted. It took bombs to deliver us.

Priestley's weekly broadcasts as Postscripts after the nine o'clock news began in 1940 and ended in 1941 as far as the British public was concerned. He continued to broadcast overseas three or four times a week. This was in addition to writing seven books and four plays. The British listener was deprived of his broadcasts because in certain respects those in authority were incapable of change. Priestley did not make propaganda, Priestley was not the Government's mouthpiece, much less the Tory Party's. He wasn't anyone's mouthpiece. He said exactly what he thought. That was the primary reason for the enormous success of his broadcasts. One had the feeling that he would have said exactly what he thought even if he'd known that it would leave him without a friend in the world. With the majority of broadcasters one sensed in the background some kind of *imprimatur*, of direction from outside, of lines being drawn, of conformation to official policy. Priestley's *imprimatur* was his own conscience. He felt that it was wrong to praise the merchant navy's heroism without also pointing out that they were shamefully underpaid and that their living and working conditions at sea were atrocious even in peacetime. This was to Priestley a matter of simple justice; to the authorities it was dangerous socialist agitation. (Incidentally, to the best of one's knowledge, Priestley had no support from any senior Labour politician.)

Asked about this, Norman Collins says:

Yes, high up in the Government there was a feeling that Jack's programmes were too socialist, that he was a dangerous fellow. Actually, he never was a socialist: he's an old-fashioned radical. It was in fact Duff Cooper, the Minister of Information, who was responsible for the Postscripts being taken off the Home Service. I protested about it, of course. To no avail, of course. It has been said that Churchill was jealous of Jack's success: I don't think that this is true. Churchill never listened to any broadcasts except his own. Though no doubt he shared Duff Cooper's opinions.

The broadcasts were classics of their kind. To begin with, Priestley had the perfect microphone voice: warm, relaxed, with a slight

Yorkshire intonation. The latter is important. Priestley is often described as having a strong Yorkshire accent. (And is the subject of excruciatingly amateurish mimicry by the sort of person who imagines that Yorkshiremen are not only obsessed by money but for some peculiar reason call it *brass*.) *Intonation* is the correct word, or perhaps *flavour* would be nearer. A strong Yorkshire accent over the air would be too strong, too reminiscent of the music-hall. The microphone is a great exaggerator, just as it is a great lie-detector.

Norman Collins went into the BBC during the war and produced the Postscripts. That he was an old friend of Priestley's and fully in rapport with him may indeed have been contributory to their success. For Norman Collins knew – as a certain type of producer does not – when to give a broadcaster his head. 'Jack would come into Broadcasting House late on Saturday night,' Norman Collins says,

with his suitcase and typewriter, and on Sunday at 2.30 pm he'd sit down at his typewriter with cotton wool in his ears and bash out the Sunday Home Service typescript. He'd put the pages of the script together then bash out another of the same length for North America. He'd finish the Home Service script for about 4.30 pm and the North American script for about 6.30 pm. It was almost uncanny to watch ... Then he'd have a drink and broadcast the Home Service piece. Then at 2.30 am he'd do the other. I can't remember that there was ever any need to revise the scripts. His attitude towards the finished piece was: 'Why should I read through what I've written? I've written it.'

Priestley also had all the other essential qualities of the great broadcaster. His stage experience had taught him timing, expression, pace, and the art of writing for the ear. His scripts would now have only historical interest: it might almost be said that if they read well, if they compared now with his published essays as literature, they wouldn't have been any good as scripts. They were pieces of first-rate craftsmanship and they made him a public figure, gave him fame which he did not altogether relish. They were an invaluable and unique contribution to the war effort, they gave heart to the nation, but he took no particular pleasure in them:

They were nothing more than spoken essays, designed to have a very broad and classless appeal. I meant what I said in them of course: a man is a fool if he tries to cheat the microphone ... No doubt I have the right voice and manner, but then so had plenty of other men. I didn't see then – and I don't see now – what all the fuss was about. To this day middle-aged or elderly men shake my hand and tell me what a ten minute talk about ducks on a pond, or a pie in a shop window meant to them, as if I had given them *King Lear* or the *Eroica*. I have found myself tied, like a man to a gigantic balloon, to one of those bogus reputations that only the mass media know how to inflict ...

I may add, however, that though I personally listened to them and enjoyed them, they had no effect upon me whatever as propaganda. Like everyone I knew of military age, I didn't need to be inspired to serve in the Armed Forces. It was a dirty job which had to be done: in the meantime one was glad of all the entertainment one could get. As far as I could work it out at that age (I was eighteen at the outbreak of war) the nation wasn't fighting for anything but survival. Nazi occupation – the only alternative to fighting – was unthinkable. About our war aims, having had the benefit of our fathers' experience, we were quietly determined. There would be a change. We honestly didn't expect great things from the change: but any change from the middle of 1939 would be a change for the better.

Looking back, one often wonders if Priestley wasn't far less cynical than we were, if it wouldn't have been preferable for him to have regarded himself as an observer or an entertainer. He had done enough service in the First World War, he owed the State nothing.

Of the seven books he wrote during the war a typical title is *The Man-Power Story*. This is not to denigrate them. They were written for a special purpose at a special time, they were part of Priestley's war service, they were written as a duty. But nothing about Priestley is as simple as it appears. *Daylight on Saturday*, for example, a novel about an aircraft factory, is readable to this day. It isn't purely ephemeral, its interest isn't purely historical. It's beautifully constructed, the characters stay in one's mind long after one has read it, and one remembers again the atmosphere of the Second World War, lives again in those days of hope:

And out they came into the daylight, blinking, chattering, grumbling, laughing, sniffing and tasting the cool air. It was a misty afternoon in early November. The sunlight was weak and watery, no more than a little pale silver in that green hollow. The blue and gold Saturdays of summer were a long way off. There were sodden dead leaves plastered like handbills on all the walls. The western sky was sagging under a load of rain. There was no wind, and the long line of buses rumbling up began to pollute the air. But the sun was there, and so was the honest daylight; and this was Saturday ...

Cheviot, the Managing Director and the central figure of the book, is leaving the factory for an even more important job. But in spirit he won't leave them:

There could be for him now no cosy settling down, no easy acceptance of bribe or pension from the moneyed interests ... no comfortable pretence that the people must naturally live on the other side of a high wall. He had to see them through. He had to labour as hard with them producing the things of peace as he had done producing the instruments of war ...

Perhaps this idealism seems naïve now, but I quote from *Daylight on Saturday* for a special reason. I came across it on the shelves of the Woking Public Library. It was published in 1944, and was a rebound copy. It would have been issued at least fifty times before rebinding and would have been issued – that is, read – at least some fifty times after rebinding. I have checked upon it in the six months since I first noticed it, and it never stays long upon the shelves. I record this not as a literary judgement but simply as a personal observation. Of one thing I am certain: none of the hundred readers of the novel read it out of historical interest. The novel is still alive as a novel. One can't argue with the verdict of the Common Reader.

The plays – *Goodnight, Children, They Came to a City, Desert Highway* and *How Are They At Home?* – have had no such continuing life. (Though if they had had, it would have been to Priestley's benefit; as he remarked to me once rather bitterly, people don't pay to borrow books, but they do pay for theatre seats.) *Goodnight, Children*, a good-natured satire on the BBC, opened at the New Theatre in February 1942 after a long provincial tour and was withdrawn after a short run. It is easy to be wise after the event, but a play satirizing the peacetime BBC would appear to have been doomed from the start. All other considerations aside, the BBC in wartime was no more to be satirized than the ARP or the National Fire Service. *They Came to a City* was tried out at the Bradford Civic Theatre and came to London in 1943, and had a long run at the Globe Theatre. It may be summarized as a dramatic interpretation of Priestley's dreams of a just society. *Desert Highway*, which had its first London production in February 1944, had as its subject a representative group of British soldiers facing death in the desert. It reached back into time to show the timelessness of the great issues of life and death. *How Are They At Home?* was produced at the Apollo in May 1944, answered the question in the title with great cheerfulness and without telling any lies. It was written as a comedy to be produced by ENSA – a message from home, a diversion which avoided equally the vapid and the portentous – and as such it was received.

The beliefs which sustained Priestley during the war years are most clearly exemplified in *They Came to a City*. The play opens with a mixed group outside a city. They are not dead. They are not dreaming, but they are removed from the constraints of time and place, they came to the city. The city is the realization of the dream we all had then of the just society. Some of the characters stay, happy and fulfilled for the first time in their lives. Some reject it angrily. Others leave it reluctantly; the memory of what they've seen there may change their lives. Joe the stoker, the discontented wanderer, leaves reluctantly, driven by the conviction that it's his duty to carry the message of the city to the world. He expects to go into the world alone; Alice, with whom he's fallen in love, has evidently stayed in the city. She joins him at the last moment, as the gates are closing:

Joe (*rising with urgency*): No, no. Don't you see – somebody's got to go back.
Alice: No, I don't see. Some of them have gone back, haven't they?
Joe: Of course they have. I expected that. Cudworth's gone back, Mrs Stritton's gone back and taken her husband with her – poor devil. Sir George and Lady What's-It have gone, even though Lady What's-It had to lose her precious daughter. Yes, they've all gone. And what good is it going to do anybody that they have gone? If they ever say a word about this place, they'll swear blind that it's terrible. So somebody's got to go back and tell the truth about it.
Alice: And that must be the bloke I go and fall for and tack on to. It just would have to be.

Joe: Yes, it must. That's just what it must be.
Alice: All right, I was trying to be funny. Tell me what you mean?
Joe: I mean, you wouldn't want a chap who could keep this to himself.

It's the note of simple idealism again. Joe believes in the brotherhood of man, believes that the world can be made a better place. If that belief is simple-minded rather than simple, then most of us were simple-minded. We did have a vision of Priestley's city. We did try to share it. Though, as I have indicated before, we weren't quite as whole-hearted or consistent as Priestley. I can still remember how quickly my belief in the City evaporated after seeing the première of the play at the Bradford Civic Playhouse. It was solid enough in the theatre: it evaporated outside in the real city.

After the war, indeed, Priestley was appointed UK Delegate to the UNESCO conferences and tried to take an active hand in building the city. Again, those were the days of hope. Priestley had no relish for public life, no enjoyment of the dreary minutiae of committee work, no need or desire for public acclaim or official position. But he did have a vision of UNESCO as nourishing a true international culture, nourishing all the arts, enriching all our lives and, in particular, of it removing the theatre from the gaming-house world. 'I felt strongly,' he said to me in 1977,

that UNESCO ought to have had quite a different organisation. I felt that it should have a small but efficient headquarters in Paris which would employ a number of temporary teams to do various jobs. As it was it showed the usual bureaucratic weaknesses. I believe it is now chiefly employed dealing with education in the third world, but originally we were chiefly concerned with cultural exchanges between more advanced nations.

The note of disillusionment is unmistakable. Later he was to put it even more explicitly in *Outcries and Asides*:

When you are very widely known as a writer – as I used to be but am no longer now – you are cajoled, persuaded, pressed to do a lot of things you don't want to do. You sign petitions, join deputations, address meetings, talk on radio or appear on television, when you would rather be working or idling at home. This is bad enough but it is even worse when writers who have refused to do things they didn't want to do, who have steadily remained working or idling at home, not putting themselves out for anybody, are praised for their dedication, their integrity, their professional purity – and often by the very people who insisted upon dragging you away from your fireside to make a public show of yourself. So – advice to a young writer: Don't do a dam'd thing for anybody ...

In the winter of 1944–5 it was evident that victory was on the way, that the worst pressures were over. What he had written up to 1944 had represented his deepest beliefs and his standards of craftsmanship had never relaxed. He had never ceased to be a creative writer, the lonely impulse of delight had always been present. Yet essentially he had been a committed writer – committed not in any political sense but committed in the sense that the purpose of his writing was to help win the war. He had been a volunteer, not a conscript; but he had not been writing for himself. He had been writing for the nation. Now he was writing for himself. His deeper part of his mind took over, the being and making part.

'I wrote this play at top speed,' he said afterwards in the preface, 'finishing it within a week.' No London theatre was available, so it had its première in Moscow in 'the summer of 1945, simultaneously by two different companies'. This was the point at which Priestley should have recognized that some things about the English ruling classes had not changed. The Russians, whatever might be said about their system of government, considered the theatre to be important. They actually took it seriously. They took writers seriously. They were the engineers of the soul, the shapers of the future. A new play of the quality of *An Inspector Calls* by a dramatist of the stature of Priestley was a national event.

For the British Government a play was a diversion, no part of the serious business of life. It might under certain circumstances have propaganda value but even about this there were reservations. Propaganda, it was felt, was the business of the politicians, working through the proper channels. It had to be sensible, it had to be down-to-earth, it had to conform to ruling-class values. Above all, it hadn't to be intellectual. It was essentially a matter of taking out of stock the time-hallowed concepts, inserting a few references to bring them up to date, and rearranging them into forms which could contain nothing to which any reasonable person would take exception and nothing which would make anyone think.

When I refer to the ruling classes I don't of course refer only to the Conservatives. The Labour members of the Government – who were at this time enjoying their first taste of real power and who were learning fast how to master the intricacies of bureaucracy – had an equal indifference to the arts and to any kind of thinking which did not directly serve the interests of the class which they represented. (Later the only class they would represent would be themselves, but that is another story.) If anything, their feelings towards the arts were of active hatred. The Conservatives merely wanted to return to their dream world, to take their part once again in the easy ritual of traditional British life so rudely interrupted by the war. There were even a few among them who were devoted to the arts; these were regarded with an amused tolerance.

All this is besides the point. It is very unlikely that any member of the Government would have been able to perceive the importance of *An Inspector Calls*. It is even more unlikely that they would have seen how vital it was that a theatre should be found for it. For none of them would have understood it. (To be entirely fair, none but a tiny minority of those who ran the British theatre would have understood it either.)

It should be made plain that there is nothing difficult about *An Inspector Calls*. It isn't abstract, it isn't symbolic, it isn't experimental. It's a straightforward three-act play with one set, and the action is continuous. Wherever it has been produced – and it has been produced, and continues to be produced, all over the world – audiences have not found it difficult. (In 1977 alone it had sixty-seven performances in England and 133 abroad.) If it puzzled them, if they found it difficult to follow, I wouldn't be writing about it now. Audiences don't go to the theatre to improve their minds, but to be entertained, to be taken out of themselves.

All three acts of *An Inspector Calls* take place in the dining-room of the Birlings' house in Brumley, an industrial city in the North Midlands on a spring evening in 1912. (Strangely enough, although I've seen the play in two stage productions and the film version, I had always assumed that the place was Yorkshire. It doesn't really matter: for each member of the audience it will be a different place – the place they know the best.)

The stage directions are worth quoting, if only to demonstrate how thoroughly Priestley knew his business as a technician. The shifts from act to act within the same set, giving a different viewpoint, are tricky, as Basil Dean, who produced the play at the New Theatre in October 1946, rather ruefully testifies:

The dining-room of a fairly large suburban house, belonging to a prosperous manufacturer. It has good solid furniture of the period. The general effect is substantial and heavily comfortable, but not cosy and homelike. (If a realistic set is used, then it should be swung back, as it was in the Old Vic production at the New Theatre. By doing this, you can have the dining-table centre downstage during Act I, when it is needed there, and then, swinging back, can reveal the fireplace for Act II, and then for Act III can show a small table with telephone on it, downstage of fireplace; and by this time the dining-table and its chairs have moved well upstage. Producers who wish to avoid this tricky business, which involves two re-settings of the scene and some very accurate adjustments of the extra flats necessary, would be well advised to dispense with an ordinary realistic set, if only because the dining-table becomes a nuisance. The lighting should be pink and intimate until the Inspector arrives, and then it should be brighter and harder.)

At rise of curtain, the four Birlings and Gerald are seated at the table, with Arthur Birling at one end, his wife at the other, Eric downstage, and Sheila and Gerald seated upstage. Edna, the parlour-maid, is just clearing the table, which has no cloth, of dessert plates and champagne glasses, etc., and then replacing them with a decanter of port, cigar box and cigarettes. Port glasses are already on the table. All five are in evening dress of the period, the men in tails and white ties, not dinner-jackets. Arthur Birling is a heavy-looking, rather portentous man in his middle fifties with fairly easy manners but rather provincial in his speech. His wife is about fifty, a rather cold woman and her husband's social superior. Sheila is a pretty girl in her early twenties, very pleased with life and rather excited. Gerald Croft is an attractive chap about thirty, rather too manly to be a dandy but very much the easy well-bred young man-about-town. Eric is in his early twenties, not quite at ease, half shy, half assertive. At the moment they have all had a good dinner, are celebrating a special occasion, and are pleased with themselves.

They are indeed pleased with themselves until the conversation comes to – the use of the phrase is inevitable – the first dangerous corner:

Birling: Oh – come, come – I'm treating Gerald like one of the family. And I'm sure he won't object.
Sheila (*with mock aggressiveness*): Go on, Gerald – just you object!

Gerald (*smiling*): Wouldn't dream of it. In fact, I insist upon being one of the family now. I've been trying long enough, haven't I? (*As she does not reply, with more insistence*) Haven't I? You know I have.

Mrs Birling (*smiling*): Of course she does.

Sheila (*half serious, half playful*): Yes – except for all last summer, when you never came near me, and I wondered what had happened to you.

The dangerous corner is somehow negotiated. Birling's self-satisfaction increases. This is the spring of 1912, he is a solid and prosperous citizen in a solid and prosperous age, his daughter has made a good match with the son of his chief business rival, he is climbing higher and higher, sure of each step, climbing from a secure base:

Birling: I'm delighted about this engagement and I hope it won't be too long before you're married. And I want to say this. There's a good deal of silly talk about these days – *but* – and I speak as a hardheaded business man, who has to take risks and know what he's about – I say, you can ignore all this silly pessimistic talk. When you marry, you'll be marrying at a very good time. Yes, a very good time – and soon it'll be an even better time. Last month, just because the miners came out on strike, there's a lot of wild talk about possible labour trouble in the near future. Don't worry. We've passed the worst of it. We employers at last are coming together to see that our interests – and the interests of Capital – are properly protected. And we're in for a time of steadily increasing prosperity.

Gerald: I believe you're right, sir.

Eric: What about war?

Birling: Glad you mentioned it, Eric. I'm coming to that. Just because the Kaiser makes a speech or two, or a few German officers have too much to drink and begin talking nonsense, you'll hear some people say that war's inevitable. And to that I say – fiddlesticks! The Germans don't want war. Nobody wants war, except some half-civilised folks in the Balkans. And why? There's too much at stake these days. Everything to lose and nothing to gain by war.

An objection to this might well be – and it is made very amusingly in Claud Cockburn's *Best-Sellers* – that we've heard this before. One answer to that objection is that it isn't an objection which has ever been made by any audience. The most cogent answer, however, is that Birling is speaking in 1912 and he is a successful British business-man and totally ignorant of political and historical realities. And he is now within reach of perfect happiness, he is about to climb out of the middle classes, to realize the dream of every successful British businessman. The ladies leave the table, the men settle down to the gravely grotesque ritual – a daft kind of Holy Communion – with port and cigars, and Birling tells Gerald a secret:

> You see, I was Lord Mayor here two years ago when Royalty visited us. And I've always been regarded as a sound useful party man. So – well – I gather there's a very good chance of a knighthood – so long as we behave ourselves, don't get into the police courts or start a scandal – eh? (*Laughs complacently*)

Birling adds that Gerald can drop a hint to his mother. 'And you can promise her that we'll try to keep out of trouble during the next few months.' The point of this is that they are all absolutely impreg-nable. The little joke, indeed, increases Birling's self-satisfaction still further. He becomes serious, a thoughtful and sensible fellow, a deep thinker in his way:

> Birling: ... I don't want to lecture you two young fellows again. But what so many of you don't seem to understand now, when things are so much easier, is that a man has to make his own way – has to look after himself – and his family too, of course, when he has one – and so long as he does that he won't come to much harm. But the way some of these cranks talk and write now, you'd think everybody has to look after everybody else, as if we were all mixed up together like bees in a hive – com-munity and all that nonsense. But take my word for it, you youngsters – and I've learnt in the good hard school of experi-ence – that a man has to mind his own business and look after himself and his own – and –

He is interrupted by the front door bell. An Inspector has called. He is shown in. Eric is jumpy, but Gerald and Birling are completely relaxed, mildly curious. They're not frightened of the police. The police are their protectors, but their servants first:

> *The Inspector enters, and Edna goes, closing the door after her. The Inspector need not be a big man but he creates at once an impression*

16 Scene from
Laburnum Grove,
Duchess Theatre, 1934

17 George (Edmund
Gwenn) reveals his
secret in the film of
Laburnum Grove, 1936

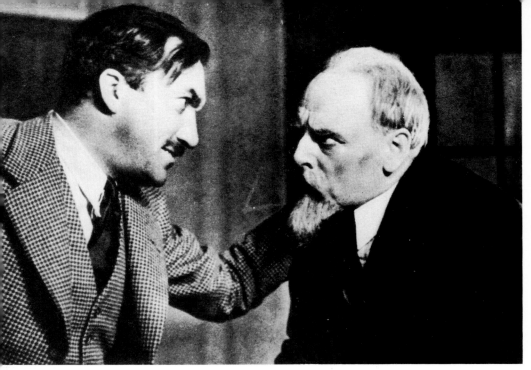

18 Wilfred Lawson and Lewis Casson in *I Have Been Here Before*, Royalty Theatre, 1937

19 Ralph Richardson (*left*) as Sam Cridley in *Bees On The Boatdeck* with Laurence Olivier as Robert Patch, Lyric Theatre, 1936

20 Priestley rehearsing the part of Henry Ormanroyd in *When We Are Married* with Patricia Hayes, St Martin's Theatre, 1938

21 Sidney Howard as the photographer in the film version of *When We Are Married*, 1943

22 Ralph Richardson in the title role of *Johnson Over Jordan*, 1939

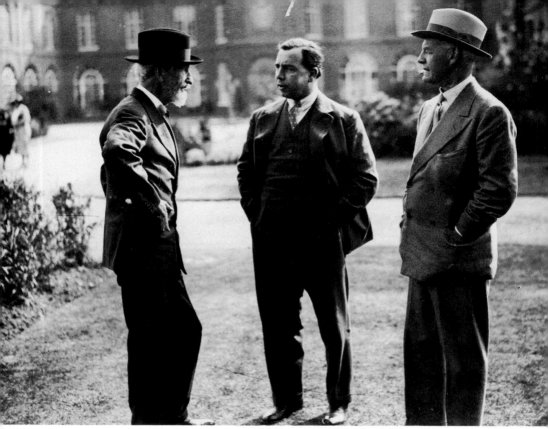

23 (*Left to right*) Graham Cunningham, Priestley and John Galsworthy, c. 1936

24 Broadcasting a Sunday evening 'Postscript', 1940

25 Visiting a miner's home, 1941

26 Film version of *They Came To A City*, 1945

27 Julian Mitchell, Ralph Richardson, Harry Andrews and Alec Guinness in *An Inspector Calls*, Old Vic, 1946

28 Sybil Thorndike and Lewis Casson in *The Linden Tree*, Duchess Theatre, 1947
29 Discussing her film *Sing As We Go* with Gracie Fields

30 Alistair Sim and Eileen
Moore in the 1953 film of
An Inspector Calls

31 With his third wife,
Jacquetta Hawkes, at
Kissing Tree House in
1964

32 Priestley at seventy-five

33 Priestley (*back row, second from left*) after receiving the Order of Merit from Her Majesty the Queen at Buckingham Palace on 17 November 1977

of massiveness, solidity and purposefulness. He is a man in his fifties, dressed in a plain darkish suit of the period. He speaks carefully, weightily, and has a disconcerting habit of looking hard at the person he addresses before actually speaking.

He drops his bombshell almost immediately:

Inspector: I'd like some information, if you don't mind, Mr Birling. Two hours ago a young woman died in the Infirmary. She'd been taken there this afternoon because she'd swallowed a lot of strong disinfectant. Burnt her inside out, of course.

Death and pain have entered the dining-room. Eva Smith, it is discovered, was one of the ringleaders of a strike at Birling's factory. She struck for an extra half-crown a week and Birling sacked her. He can't understand the drift of the Inspector's questions but the questions continue, quietly and remorselessly.

They are all involved in her death. Birling sacked her in the first place. She found a good job in a shop; then Sheila, in a moment of pique, had her sacked from that. Sheila, who has thought of herself as being on the girl's side, has been responsible for bringing her nearer to an agonizing death. She doesn't attempt to justify herself. She is desperately ashamed:

Sheila: ... Oh – why had this to happen?
Inspector (*sternly*): That's what I asked myself to-night when I was looking at that dead girl. And then I said to myself: 'Well, we'll try to understand why it had to happen.' And that's why I'm here, and why I'm not going until I know *all* that happened. Eva Smith lost her job with Birling and Company because the strike failed and they were determined not to have another one. At last she found another job – under what name I don't know – in a big shop, and had to leave there because you were annoyed with yourself and passed the annoyance on to her. Now she had to try something else. So first she changed her name to Daisy Renton –

Gerald is startled at the name. He too has helped to kill Eva Smith. She had been his mistress; and when he was tired of her, he rejected her. He used her. And Mrs Birling has helped to kill her too. She refused her the aid she could have given from the Brumley Women's

Charity Organization. And in so doing killed her own grandchild; her son Eric was the father of the girl's unborn child.

The Inspector now pronounces the verdict:

Inspector: This girl killed herself – and died a horrible death. But each of you helped to kill her. Remember that. Never forget it. (*He looks from one to the other of them carefully*) But then I don't think you ever will. Remember what you did, Mrs Birling. You turned her away when she most needed help. You refused her even the pitiable little bit of organised charity you had in your power to grant her. Remember what you did –

Eric (*unhappily*): My God – I'm not likely to forget.

Inspector: Just used her for the end of a stupid drunken evening, as if she was an animal, a thing, not a person. No, you won't forget. (*He looks at Sheila*)

Sheila (*bitterly*): I know. I had her turned out of a job. I started it.

Inspector: You helped – but didn't start it. (*Rather savagely, to Birling*) You started it. She wanted twenty-five shillings a week instead of twenty-two and sixpence. You made her pay a heavy price for that. And now she'll make you pay a heavier price still.

Birling (*unhappily*): Look, Inspector – I'd give thousands – yes, thousands –

Inspector: You're offering the money at the wrong time, Mr Birling. (*He makes a move as if concluding the session, possibly shutting up notebook, etc. Then he surveys them sardonically*) No, I don't think any of you will forget. Nor that young man, Croft, though he at least had some affection for her and made her happy for a time. Well, Eva Smith's gone. You can't do her any more harm. And you can't do her any good now, either. You can't even say 'I'm sorry, Eva Smith.'

Sheila (*who is crying quietly*): That's the worst of it.

Inspector: But just remember this. One Eva Smith has gone – but there are millions and millions and millions of Eva Smiths and John Smiths still left with us, with their lives, their hopes and fears, their suffering, and chance of happiness, all intertwined with our lives, with what we think and say and do. We don't live alone. We are members of one body. We are responsible for each other. And I tell you that the time will soon come when, if men will not learn that lesson, then they will be taught it in fire and blood and anguish . . .

That isn't the end. The end is still to come and when it does come it isn't the end, but the beginning of another play which each of the audience will write for themselves as they leave the theatre. What happens in that play which begins after the final curtain of Act Three is infinitely more terrible than anything which has gone before. But the message of *An Inspector Calls* is simple: *We don't live alone. We are members of one body. We are responsible for each other.* It is so simple that only a great writer would have the courage to make it his central theme. And it offers a very easy – in fact, cheap – explanation for its success behind the Iron Curtain. Being all responsible for each other is what communism's supposed to be all about. One can't see how the Russians could have refused to produce it. Any official who objected to it being produced would have been accused of objecting to a moving and powerful exposition of the high ideal of the brotherhood of man. But – though they would have kept very quiet about it – there would have been those behind the Iron Curtain who would have objected to the play. For a start, all its characters are human beings. And it isn't committed except in the sense of being dramatically committed, committed to entertainment. But the objection which any intelligent person in authority in a totalitarian state would make would go beyond this. The Inspector's final speech is more than a statement. It is also a question which is asked of each member of the audience. There is no hint of the question in the words of the speech, but it is absolutely explicit: how far is it true of this society that we are members of one body? Just as there is an even more powerful play beyond the play, there are even more powerful words beyond the words. The impact of what is heard and seen in *An Inspector Calls* derives from what is not heard and seen.

In Priestley's novel *Bright Day*, published in 1946, there is this note to the reader:

Because this novel is written in the first person and its action swings from the West Riding I once knew to the contemporary film world, a special word of caution is probably necessary. This work is pure fiction, containing no autobiographical material, no portraits of actual persons living or dead, no reporting of scenes ever visible to my outward eye. I beg the reader to accept this not as a mere formality but as a solemn assurance.

If he meant that the novel isn't autobiographical, all this is quite true. Gregory Dawson, the film-writer hero and narrator, isn't J. B. Priestley. His life, though similar to J. B. Priestley's life, isn't the same life. The characters are fictitious, though real people in one way or another were their starting-off points. The scenes which were visible to Priestley's outward eye include his bedroom in Bradford (*Margin Released*, pp. 26–7), which may be compared with the description of Gregory Dawson's bedroom in Brigg Terrace, Bruddersford (*Bright Day*, pp. 16–17). And again and again the Bruddersford scenes and indeed the Yorkshire scenes were visible to my outward eye. Most of the city scenes are visible now only to the eye of memory; the countryside remains. And in fact the novel is in part the traditional *bildungroman*, the story of a young man growing up, learning about his vocation and learning, learning about love. (Or rather, one should say, beginning the process of learning.) It isn't autobiographical because no true novelist can ever bear to be autobiographical. (And, as I've already stated, *Midnight on the Desert* and *Rain upon Godshill* aren't really true autobiographies: a true autobiography reveals all, hides nothing). *Bright Day* is roughly comparable to *David Copperfield* and, like *David Copperfield*, was written in the author's maturity. Priestley's first novel wasn't autobiographical, wasn't any kind of *bildungroman*. A true novelist is economical with his material and in any case wouldn't be interested in himself as a subject. In maturity one's younger self can be seen at the proper distance, it becomes the starting-off point.

Bright Day was, until *The Image Men*, Priestley's favourite novel. He says in *Margin Released*:

I did not fail the idea with which I began, in spite of considerable technical difficulties, the constant shift of time, atmosphere, tone. Another is although the story is not at all autobiographical – the first person narrator, Gregory Dawson, is a writer, it is true, but both his work and his attitude towards it are quite different from mine – I was able to recreate, in the scenes recollected from Dawson's youth, something of the life I have known before 1914, and not, I believe, without colour, warmth and tenderness. And it does seem to me even now, though of course I may still be flattering myself, that I did succeed in weaving into one fabric many different fibres: Dawson's personal history and that of the Alington family, the change in the social scene, the cronies that passing time leaves behind. It may be all a little naïve for our most brilliant contemporary minds; but then so am I. And here for once, try as I might, I cannot grumble, for *Bright Day* was generally received as I hoped it would be, and among the many people who read the book were some I was delighted to please. One of them was Jung, who wrote me a long letter about it ...

I still remember the shock which the book gave me in 1946. I still have the Penguin edition, bought in 1951 for half-a-crown. I was a librarian then; I could easily have borrowed the book. But it was one of those books, like Rilke's *Sonnets to Orpheus*, which one had to possess, to return to again and again. And it was the book which made me take Priestley seriously as a novelist. (I'm talking here about my younger self.) It was not only that I identified with the hero in his Bruddersford period, knew his Bruddersford and knew his Yorkshire: it was his technique, his superb handling of the transitions of time and place and mood which compelled my admiration, if admiration isn't too tepid a word.

Gregory Dawson, the hero, is working to a deadline to finish a film script in a Cornish hotel. ' "That's the place for you, Greg," he said. "Nothing to do but work. They'll give you a room about the size of Stage Four. The food's dull and there isn't much of it, and most of the people there are just waiting for death. So you'll be hungry and bored, and you'll have to work ..." ' There are about forty people staying at the hotel; he doesn't want to mix with them, but notices in the dining-room a prosperous-looking couple in their sixties who seem vaguely familiar. He recognizes them eventually as Malcolm and Eleanor Nixey, who he hasn't seen for more than thirty years. What releases the memories, the equivalent of Proust's Madeline, is the slow movement of Schubert's B Flat Major Trio; Gregory has challenged the two young girls in the hotel trio to give him some real music.

A few moments later, when the 'cello went wandering to murmur its regret and the violin with its piercing sweetness curved and rocked in the same little tune, I was far away, deep in a lost world and a lost time. I was back again – young Gregory Dawson, eighteen, shy but sprawling – in the Alingtons' drawing-room in Bruddersford, before the First World War, years and years ago, half a good lifetime away.

Gregory sets himself to recapturing the past. It begins in his last year at school. His mother and father die in India within a week of one another and he goes to live with his Uncle Miles, his mother's only brother, and his wife, Aunt Hilda:

It was arranged between us that when I finally left school I should go to live with them in Bruddersford, where of course I had stayed before. If I still wanted to go to Cambridge, they told me, then they would see that I went there; which meant, I knew, that the responsibility would be chiefly theirs, for my father had left me very little. But I had told them already that now I did not want to go to Cambridge, that it did not seem to matter any more. I knew what I did want to do, sooner or later, and that was to write ... I dropped a hint or two of this ambition to my aunt and uncle, and they pointed out very sensibly that they could not turn me into a writer, I would have to turn myself into one, and that in the meantime, if I did not want to go to university, I might as well learn something useful and also earn a little money. So we agreed that after the holidays Uncle Miles should try to find me some sort of job in the local trade, the wool trade. And that is how I came to live in Bruddersford, to work in the office of Hawes and Company, and to know the Alingtons and their friends – and Malcolm and Eleanor Nixey.

From this point, with no hint of strain, no sense of agonized contrivance, Gregory is two persons in two places, his younger self in Bruddersford, his middle-aged self in the dreary Cornish hotel. The younger Gregory, who dreams of being a writer, lives in a world of magic:

No Bruddersford man could be exiled from the uplands and blue air; he always had one foot on the heather; he had only to pay his tuppence on the tram and then climb for half an hour to hear the larks and curlews, to feel the old rocks warming in the sun, to see the harebells trembling in the shade. And on the days when the hills were bright in the sunlight, the streets in the centre of Bruddersford, underneath their shifting canopy of smoke, seemed to me to have a curious and charming atmosphere of their own, a peculiar alternation of dim gold and grey gloom ...

There is magic in the countryside, magic in the city; and over and above it all magic in people. And I remembered now how I was haunted during those first months in Bruddersford. From Brigg Terrace the straightest way in or out of the city was along the rather dreary Wabley Road, where the tall trams went swaying and groaning ... And there I noticed, going into town and coming out of it, a group that varied in size, ranging from three people to eight or nine, but that always had the same group identity in my mind, and that always suggested the mysterious and fascinating unknown tribe and hinted at a life infinitely richer than my own ...

These are the Alingtons. There's the father, tall, casually dressed, with an intelligent and humorous face, the mother, three pretty daughters, girls to dream about, a noisy young son of about Gregory's age, and a young man who appears to be attached to one of the girls.

Purely by chance Gregory is employed as junior clerk at the office of Hawes and Company and discovers that the father of the magic family is the head of the firm or, to be more accurate, in charge of the Bruddersford branch of the firm. He is drawn into the magic circle, the future opens out before him, life makes huge promises, not least the promise of love. And his world is 'secure, rich and warm', and the promises are all to be trusted. His friend Jock Barniston is 'one of those very rare persons ... who do little or nothing of any consequence, make no effort to attract attention, seem content with the commonplace, and yet leave with everybody who knows them an enduring impression of integrity and strength, of vast unused powers, of carelessly veiled greatness'. Jock warns him about the Alingtons:

The Alingtons are an amusing, rather clever, very charming family, and I'm fond of 'em all. But don't try to make them add up to anything more than that. Don't turn them, somewhere at the back of your mind, into something they aren't and wouldn't pretend to be. Don't make everything stand or fall by them. Switch off the magic, which comes from you and not from them. Don't cast a spell over yourself and imagine that they're doing it. Take them in your stride, and don't fix anything. See what I mean?

But Gregory doesn't listen to Jock, he makes too large an emotional investment in the Alingtons: *It is the bright day that brings forth the adder.* Two world wars and thirty years later he is left an empty man.

He finishes the film script he has come to Cornwall to write, the script is accepted enthusiastically, he finds himself in London after a disillusioning meeting with Bridget Alington, arranged behind his back by a well-meaning friend. He hates London and he hates his life:

It was only a quarter to six and I didn't want to go to my flat. That scene I had to re-write could wait until after dinner or if necessary until the morning. A bus took me down Park Lane and along the Green Park end of Piccadilly, and then I walked as far as the Hippodrome, went up Charing Cross Road, and then at Cambridge Circus I turned down Shaftesbury Avenue. I did this with some vague idea of seeing a play or a film, but there didn't seem to be anything new I wanted to see. The early evening crowds were swarming, especially along Coventry Street. London looked horrible, like the shabbier side of some third-rate American city ... It was a hellish huddle of nasty trading, of tired pleasure-seeking, of entertainment without art, of sex without passion and joy, of life buzzing and swarming without hope and vision. London could take it. But how much more of this could it take?

And then the two stories become one story, past and present converge, and there is hope again, he isn't absolutely certain he'll be happy but he is certain that he'll be alive. And that is the keynote of the novel. Technically it is in my opinion the most accomplished of all his novels. One can bring to mind no other living writer – except Anthony Powell – who has the ability to so fully bring the past to life within the narrative whilst at the same time keeping the narrative within the present. The effect is not of being shown two separate parts of his life, but the whole life. And throughout there is enormous warmth, enormous emotional vitality, and, rarest of all, compassion. There are no villains. Even the Nixeys, who the young Gregory believes destroyed the Alingtons, are not to be seen in such simple terms:

'We're leaving in the morning, and probably you and I won't meet again. So I'm going to risk telling you something that nobody else knows.' There was no warmth in her tone, no hint of any emotion in her voice: she was cool and incisive. 'It's all ancient history, but as we seem to have been thinking about it, we might as well get it straight. You still think – as that Alington child said that night – that I deliberately took Ben Kerry away from her sister for a little amusement, just grabbed him to pass the time, don't you? Of course you do ... That's the kind of thing I might easily have done at that time. But this was quite different. There wasn't any grabbing and amusement. I was in love with Ben. It was the first and last time I ever was in love. That girl – or any other girl that age – couldn't have begun to understand what I felt about him. I was ready to give up everything for him. When he was killed, just after we spent his last leave together, I thought I'd go mad. And I've never really forgotten a single second of the time Ben and I spent together. That's why I said you weren't the only person here with a memory.'

He has until this moment seen Eleanor Nixey as sterile and empty and destructive, cold and greedy and hard – the person who, together with her husband, wrecked the lives of the Alingtons, disrupted the magic circle. Now he sees her as a person, a giver, as much a victim as the Alingtons. And she tells him something about Malcolm which makes him see Malcolm too as a victim. The Nixeys are struggling and imperfect, at the mercy of huge forces outside themselves and within themselves. They are human. And all this can only be understood by a mature man; which is yet another reason why *Bright Day* is so deeply satisfying and why Priestley didn't make a novel like it his first novel.

In 1947, *The Linden Tree* had its first production. The title was taken from a play he had written in Arizona eight years earlier but had, on his wife's advice, put aside. 'There was nothing really wrong with it: a sensible and solid play was in the making there; but she was quite right: it belonged to some other man.' The new play had no resemblance whatever to the rejected play and was written in ten days in the bitter winter of 1947. The year was bitter in more ways than one: the nation was – and this is a statement of fact – beginning to be disillusioned with the Labour Government. The nation had voted for a better society, a society in which each could say, to quote Inspector Goole, 'We are members of one body.' It hadn't voted for continued food rationing, fuel rationing, or power cuts. *The Linden Tree* is an affirmation of faith. It is not in the Labour Government – which it regarded as merely one of the means, a grossly limited one – to an end. It is an affirmation of faith in the proposition that we don't live just for ourselves, but for something outside ourselves, that if we are to be more than talking animals, we must give ourselves and not count the cost, we mustn't take the easy way.

When the play opens, Professor Linden, who teaches history in

a red-brick university in the Midlands, has been politely asked to
retire. He will be no worse off financially. His wife and family all
want him to leave. Only his youngest daughter, Dinah, is on his side.
There is no reason why he shouldn't leave. He's sixty-five and
entitled to retirement in any case. He says that he likes the 'glum
murky old place' but his wife doesn't. He can't hope at his age for
any sort of promotion or even to alter things very much. But, as
he puts it to his friend Lockhart, he is going to fight:

I was telling my family, who don't care a damn, that we're trying to
do a wonderful thing here. And so we are. But somehow not in a wonderful
way. There's a kind of grey chilly hollowness inside, where there ought
to be gaiety, colour, warmth, vision. Sometimes our great common enterprise seems only a noble skeleton, as if the machines had already sucked
the blood and marrow out of it. My wife and family tell me to go away
and enjoy myself. Doing what? Watching the fire die out of the heart,
and never even stooping to blow? Here in Burmanley – with Dinah and
her kind – and a few friends and allies – I can still blow a little – brighten
an ember or two.

If he stays, it will be to face implacable opposition from the new
Vice-Chancellor. Linden says:

He's an educationalist. He educationalizes – in quite a big dashing sort
of way. It's something quite different from educating people – newer and
much better. They'll probably have machines to do it soon, when they
can import them from America. Two of my oldest friends here – Tilley
and Clark – have already resigned. I believe he's hoping I'll go next. I won't
say I see it in his eye, because he always gives me the extraordinary impression that he has two glass eyes ...

Linden stands for different values, for the non–utilitarian values,
for individual freedom, for the disinterested quest for truth. He
stands also for human warmth, for colour and light, perhaps even
for magic. He believes that man is a spirit and not a machine. He
doesn't expect anyone to understand, he can't be sure that the social
engineers, the grey cold ones, won't win. But he can try to stop them.
In the end he's left alone with Dinah, his youngest daughter. Dinah
understands, Dinah shares his idealism. Dinah knows how to give,
Dinah knows how to love.

The play ends with Dinah and Linden. Linden's wife has left him

– which is not unreasonable in the circumstances. His son and his two other daughters have gone away. It's late at night and he's sitting alone brooding. Dinah comes down in her pyjamas and dressing gown and asks him to read to her from his book on history. As he reads to her she falls asleep. He looks at her and smiles, then, his attention having been caught by a word in the manuscript, he takes out a pen and goes to work on it as the curtain falls. It's a very quiet ending, by no means a surprise ending, with a great deal beneath the surface. Technically, only a dramatist of Priestley's experience would have had the skill or the audacity to get away with a long extract from an authentic history book which must be read as a professor of history would read it. If it isn't long enough for Dinah credibly to fall asleep, there's no point in reading it. But there's a danger that the audience may fall asleep with her.

That they kept very much awake is proved by the play's success. *The Linden Tree* ran for 422 performances. None of the plays which followed had the same success. What is heartening about that success is that it demonstrates how untrue the maxim is that no one ever went broke underestimating the taste of the public. There is, it goes without saying, no question of it not being theatrically effective. Priestley's craftsmanship cannot be faulted. But it is, more than any other of his plays, a play of ideas. The appeal is of the essential nobility of those ideas. There isn't a happy ending in the strict sense of the word. What we're presented with is an old man, against all his best interests, doing the right thing. There is nothing spectacular about his action – or rather his decision. He won't even have the glory of martyrdom. But we are uplifted by *The Linden Tree*, we are assured that man is made in God's image, not a computer's. If Priestley's father could have seen this play, one feels that this is the one of which he would have been the proudest.

Sadly, *The Linden Tree* was Priestley's last successful venture into the West End until his adaptation, with Iris Murdoch, of her novel *A Severed Head* in 1963. And an adaptation in collaboration is by no means the same thing as a new play. As far as West End management was concerned it was as if, literally, they didn't know of his existence. The word 'literally' isn't used here lightly. Only if management was completely unaware of his achievement in the theatre up to and including *The Linden Tree* can his absence from the West End be explained. But this is obviously fantastic: his plays had a continuing life in radio and TV and on the amateur stage, and he was a world figure in the theatre. The answer is that, as he himself has said, the standards of the West End are those of the gaming-house. They weren't even straightforward commercial standards. If West End managers were businessmen, then Priestley's record of solid success should have ensured them queuing at his door for a new play. They didn't. They preferred to back their almost always disastrous hunches.

Dragon's Mouth, written in collaboration with Jacquetta Hawkes and produced in 1952, was a fresh and exciting experiment – in fact a play for four characters but in evening-dress with scripts and no scenery or stage lighting, a dramatic reading. It could have been the establishment of a new dramatic form, not to replace the conventional play, but to supplement it. But any new form intended to remove one set of problems ensures another set of problems, completely unfamiliar problems, to replace them. *Dragon's Mouth* died; but the experiment was well worth making.

But it is not *Dragon's Mouth* which marks the end of a period in Priestley's life. It is the long comic novel, *Festival at Farbridge*, published in 1951. This I took at the time to be no more and no less than a light-hearted novel, a pure entertainment. Technically – I was planning my first novel then – I was enormously impressed by it. I was astounded by Priestley's feat of sheer organization and endurance, the way in which he handled the huge cast of characters and kept up the pace of the narrative. He didn't have walk-on parts, and there wasn't any padding. The plot seemed exuberantly complicated, surprises exploded like land-mines, but the theme was clear. The rogue, Commodore Tribe, was going to bring a festival to the sleepy town of Farbridge with the help of Theodore Jenks and Laura Casey, his two nice young assistants, and Farbridge would be a better place for it and Theodore and Laura would marry. I was then having a hard time in a bed-sitter in Kensington, having given up a safe job as a librarian to be a freelance writer. I wasn't at all well-disposed towards the Festival of Britain, but *Festival at Farbridge* made me, however briefly, understand what it ought to have been.

The Festival of Britain was, in fact, the last manifestation, the last gasp of what we had begun to hope for during the war, what we had intermittently felt during the General Election of 1945. It isn't simple to explain because people on the whole were, as always, absorbed in their own personal lives. The festival was outside their personal lives. It didn't change their lives. But there was a difference in the atmosphere. There was the feeling that things might change, that we might even hope that government would be a manifestation of the will of the people, that it wouldn't be mean and ignoble and petty-spirited, that it would encourage the life-enhancers (to use Priestley's phrase), that it would make sure that the people had something to sing about. For there had to be something better – and not merely better in material terms – than what we'd had between the wars. I hoped in 1951 that there was still some hope, that politicians might behave like civilized and reasonable human beings. I'm aware that too much must not be read into *Festival at Farbridge*. But I'm instinctively certain that, like all of us, Priestley felt hope. And after the festival there were public buildings left, an increased public support of the arts, there was a festival style established, a lack of fussiness, a lightness and cleanness of line, a sort of frivolity – but the hope ebbed away, nothing was going to be any different, it certainly wouldn't be as it was between the wars, but worse, worse in a new way. Looking back, one sees that it was the same old story. A promise was made; a promise was broken.

7

Long Indian Summer

In 1953 Priestley married Jacquetta Hawkes, an archaeologist and author of *The Land*, a tall, gravely beautiful woman whose great personal gift is a warm serenity. He is, as I have said, extremely reticent where his private life is concerned; but it is no secret that his third marriage was, and is, completely happy and fulfilling. Their relationship was from the first based on a deep intellectual and spiritual rapport, all the deeper because, on the face of it, they were at different ends of the spectrum. Yet again one must over-simplify: he stood at the emotional and creative end and she at the intellectual and analytical end. But this is to disregard the fact of his intellectual and analytical side and her emotional and creative side. As their friend Diana Collins, wife of Canon John Collins, put it: 'They're absolutely complementary. You can't imagine one without the other.' In his fifties Priestley had found personal happiness, had made a fresh start. He told Diana Collins later: 'Until I met Jacquetta, I was always looking for something, never content – in her I found what I was looking for.' And what he found was not a *folie à deux* but a *sagesse à deux* which was surely the chief source of his continuing creative energy in the years when most men's powers begin to decline.

After their marriage the Priestleys took up residence at Kissing Tree House, a beautifully proportioned Georgian house in the village of Alverston near Stratford-on-Avon. In London – which he now less and less frequently visits – Priestley continued to keep two sets of chambers in Albany. At Kissing Tree House there is an atmosphere which I have rarely met elsewhere. Comfort, warmth, tranquillity, order – all these would be part of it. A proper dignity is too, but

132

nothing has been chosen as a showpiece but simply because, whether a picture or a piece of furniture, or a piece of china, it gives lasting pleasure, it can be lived with happily. The key word for the Priestleys' home would be, I think, festivity. There is always the sense that there will be a party, a real party, not a party to pay off social obligations, a party where one will meet all the people one's been wanting to meet, a party where there'll be plenty to eat and drink but no gourmandizing or boozing because everybody's too busy talking, a party with no hangovers, a party at which delight would always be the guest of honour. All this, I felt, is chiefly the consequence of the fact that the life of the house has always been centred round hard and joyous work and that each moment in it has been lived to the full.

Journey Down a Rainbow (1955), in collaboration with Jacquetta Hawkes, marks Priestley's return to social criticism. There is no question of the rejection of the ideals of Professor Linden, his vision of the just society has not changed. But the world had changed. Hitler had been defeated; but there was a new enemy. *Journey Down a Rainbow* is the record of a trip to the USA by Priestley and his wife in 1954. It specifically isn't a travel book. As Priestley states in the preface, 'English readers have not to be conducted across the Atlantic now to observe the American style of urban life: it can be discovered in the nearest town ...' America was chosen because

if you wish as we did to compare some of the earliest men with some of the latest, to make a contrast between two very different ways of life, the American South-West offers you an opportunity not to be found elsewhere. For there, neighbouring states, are New Mexico and Texas. In New Mexico some of the earliest inhabitants of America made their homes; and their successors, the prehistoric Basket Maker and Pueblo Indians, have left in their mesa-top villages and cliff-dwellings some of the most remarkable remains of any primitive people in the world. What is more, and very important for our purpose, the modern Pueblos, a peaceful sedentary people who have never moved from their ancestral lands, still preserve much of their ancient culture, far more (as we shall see) than is generally realised by European archaeologists and prehistorians. They are still living more or less as they always did, and, in spite of all the assaults of Western civilisation, still offer us insights into prehistoric ways ...

The book is not in fact a collection of essays and notes, as Priestley with undue modesty suggests it might be. It is an organic whole, and a completely fruitful collaboration. (It should be noted as a sidelight on his character how often and how successfully Priestley has worked with others.) Like *English Journey* it is a journey throughout, whether in Texas or New Mexico, the *poésie du départ* is always there. But what the book is doing is the job which the sociologists should be doing, to examine a changing society. Looking back I don't remember that any other writer at that time was even aware that society was changing. In Britain at least it was as if time had stopped once the nation had settled down into civilian life again. The very people whose vocation it was to see the shape of our society clearly, could not be said to see the present, let alone the future. Priestley saw the future – which is now with us – summing it up in a term which has passed into the language:

I have coined some new names, and from now on I shall use them. I shall do this not only for quick convenient reference but also to avoid suggesting, even to myself, that I am merely criticising America and not contemporary Western society in general. (Though America gave us the lead, of course, and is much further along. The rest of us, half sleep-walking, totter on behind.) First then – *Admass*. This is my name for the whole system of an increasing productivity, plus inflation, plus a rising standard of material living, plus high-pressure advertising and salesmanship, plus mass communications, plus cultural democracy and the creation of the mass mind, the mass man ...

He had coined a new name (though it was Kierkegaard, more than 100 years ago, who first foresaw the emergence of mass man). And with Jacquetta Hawkes he had written a new book. He jumped on no one else's bandwaggon: he built his own. Others were to ride on the Admass bandwaggon, passing it off as their own. But no one heeded his warnings; they merely re-stated his observations when it was too late to do anything to remedy the situation.

His involvement with the Campaign for Nuclear Disarmament came in 1957, its origin being an earlier campaign against the pollution caused by nuclear tests; CND was never in terms of membership a mass movement. (It is still very much a going concern and its membership of 20,000 is now actually greater than it was at the height

of its influence.) Its annual march to the nuclear weapons establishment at Aldermaston captured the public imagination and – which
was more than could be said of the political parties – it had the active
support of the young. It was a peculiarly English movement. It was
not politically aligned – in fact, it almost split the Labour Party in
1959 – but there were certainly no Conservatives among its members.
It was not, strictly speaking, pacifist. Its aim was unilateral nuclear
disarmament, not total disarmament. (One point I myself used to
make was that the money saved by nuclear disarmament could be
spent on strengthening our non-nuclear defences.) But there were
of course among its members those who were committed to total
disarmament. Its demonstrations were non-violent; it was funda-
mentally a civilized and middle-class organization which hoped to
achieve its aims by reason and persuasion. There was a time when
it seemed to be within reach of achievement of its aim, when it
seemed to have a genuine moral force, when it seemed about to change
history without the use of violence or political intrigue. And then
something went out of it and even if one still believed in unilateral
nuclear disarmament one couldn't support it any more. Something
came into it too, completely distorting its purpose. What came into
it could have been fought against but in the fight one would have
been tainted.

And through CND Priestley and his wife made one of their most
happy and lasting friendships: with Canon John Collins of St Paul's
and his wife Diana. Significantly, the first time they came into con-
tact with him, the notion that they would be friends would have
seemed fantastic. The occasion was at a meeting against capital
punishment with Victor Gollancz in the chair. Diana Collins said:

> I took the strongest possible dislike to Jack – he was so crass and glowering
> and unhelpful. He spoke brilliantly, though. The next time we met him,
> though, the circumstances were quite the reverse. It was at his home. But
> I should really put it differently. I mean that when we really met him for
> the first time, on his own ground, we saw the real Jack. The truth is, Jack
> has a terrible mistrust of the crowd – though when he's on form he can
> really move multitudes. He doesn't basically like public speaking. He rather
> despises it. Oratory is, after all, the harlot of the arts. And Jack does have
> this outstanding honesty and integrity ... He taught me a lot about public

speaking – he says it's very easy compared with writing. He thinks that all that the public wants is to have a love affair with you. They long for rapport with you, they want their lives to be transformed ...

Canon Collins had the same impression of Priestley before he actually met him at the Albany:

The main origin of CND was three articles by Jack in the *New Statesman*. The response was so great in terms of readers' letters that the editor, Kingsley Martin, felt that it was time to start a campaign against nuclear weapons. Kingsley put my name forward as chairman and Jack said that if he was going to serve under me as chairman he wanted to meet me first and get to know me. So Diana and I did meet him; and our friendship – the friendship of the four of us – was almost like falling in love at first sight. What grew very quickly was a very close intellectual and spiritual bond ... The friendship grew in a very short time and by the end of the CND campaign the friendship didn't conclude but became closer ... The end of CND really marked the end of his active involvement in public affairs ... Though not his active *concern* ... I don't think that he really ever hoped to convert the whole nation to nuclear disarmament. But he did have some hopes that the Labour Party might be converted. We came, I believe, very near to it. Even though we didn't achieve any aim it's good to remember those days. Jack was the best of people to work with: I'd rather be with him in a crisis than anyone else I know. And he has a wonderful sense of humour, he brings one back to earth, to a sense of reality. I never expected to when I first met him, but I genuinely came to love him. I had once thought of him before I met him as anti-religious. I discovered indeed that he was anti-church but not – absolutely not – anti-religious. Not that I ever tried to convert him or have ever even contemplated his becoming converted to Christianity in the usual sense of the word ... Though my profession is conversion I've always believed that the best way to convert people is not openly to attempt to convert. We have talked very often about religion and philosophy. Our identity of outlook and purpose is far closer than it sometimes is with some of one's colleagues ... There's always been the deep-down feeling that the four of us share the things which matter the most. As for Time, I can't always follow him – but it's unthinkable that there should be no permanent and eternal value attached to human relationships, that death should be the end ... Though in part his thinking is in a line with my view of the Resurrection ... Incidentally – and this is most important – Jack has never once attempted to alter my thinking,

136

he's never done otherwise than take my position seriously. He has a rich and deep belief in the Jungian philosophy. He knows much more about Jung than I do. He believes – and this of course is to over-simplify – in Man, not Mass Man controlled by the State, but Man as part of the human race. One thing he has taught me. I don't label myself. Recently I talked about the ugly face of socialism in connection particularly with certain strikes which threatened the essential services. There was a flood of letters, half from Tories congratulating me on being converted to Toryism and half from Socialists rebuking me for having betrayed Socialism. Actually, I'd done neither. But I realise that both lots were labelling me. And I won't have it. Labels are for parcels, not human beings. And perhaps knowing Jack has helped me to speak as myself and not as a member of an organisation. I owe a great deal to him for having taught me to understand things more deeply. He doesn't believe in taking up a polarised position and neither do I . . .

Of the other side of Priestley's personality, the side that is perhaps the least understood, Canon Collins says perceptively:

Whilst being the most masculine of men, Jack has a deep understanding of women and takes great pleasure in their company. He believes very strongly in giving the female principle its proper place in our society. He believes that precisely what's wrong with our society is that it's far too much directed by the masculine principle. All men have the feminine within them and all women have the male. This has nothing whatever to do with sex in the usual sense. Jack is the man that he is, and the supreme artist that he is, because this femininity is so sensitive and so acute.

Diana Collins confirms this:

Jack says that he much prefers to talk to women than to men. And he's marvellous to talk to. He never says anything he doesn't mean. So if he says anything nice to you, he means it one hundred per cent. Of course, he'll tick you off if you say anything pretentious or false. He's much nicer with women, though, than the majority of men are. He talks about the things women are interested in – personal relationships, for example. *Human* relationships, relationships between men and women. He does talk about his work sometimes, but prefers not to on the whole . . . What impresses me is the depth of his self-knowledge. Most of us look at ourselves in a bumbling, vague way, but he looks at himself clearly and steadily. This is a source of great wisdom. Above all, he's a generous man. He's best on his own ground. He says that he's a much better host than he's a guest. He's always much happier giving than receiving. The only thing he's not keen on giving is advice, but when he does give it, it's always worth having. He's a marvellous friend – if you're a friend of his, you're a friend for life. You can always depend upon him. Our friendship is a real foursome, which is very rare. Generally one person likes only one of the other pair and puts up with their partner for their sake. It's difficult to sum up Jack – he's so many-sided. Certainly in his life joy and woe have been woven fine. He knows what suffering is. He's had a full life, though, he's had far more than most men. But there's an essay of his called *Something Else*. We're all, you see, looking for something else. Jack will always be looking for something else . . .

Possibly because he is always 'looking for something else' his intellectual energy seemed, at a time in life when most men are slowing down, positively to increase. His collection of essays, *Thoughts in the Wilderness* (1957), would in itself have made a lasting reputation for another writer. What dazzled me at the time – and still does on returning to them – is the originality and freshness of his ideas. Once again his gift is displayed of making abstract and complex ideas instantly understandable to the Common Reader. But this isn't achieved through writing down to the reader, or reducing his prose to a kind of baby-talk, but by the use of an image so arresting and so obvious that long afterwards, having used it so often, having in fact found it impossible not to use it, one is convinced that it's not Priestley's at all. The idea becomes one's own, one establishes squatters' rights. And I, for instance, have established squatters' rights in his concept of block thinking.

Neat sets of beliefs and opinions are fastened together; and you are expected to take the lot. Either live in one Block or go and find a room in the next Block. Stay in the street outside, and you will be sniped at from all the windows. A Completely Outfitted man, a good Block Thinker, would rather have a fellow from the other Block, properly Outfitted, than tolerate a ditherer without a Block and Outfit. Let him shuffle off to the wilderness where he belongs!

The sustained image is more than an embellishment to the idea, the spoonful of sugar to make the medicine go down. It *is* the idea. If it's taken away then one fails to realize that the pressure to conform comes always from the same people, that they are the enemies of liberty and of life itself. And having written this I realize what the great gift of Priestley as an essayist is. He makes the process of thought, of using one's intelligence, exciting, he is the great liberator.

It was *Thoughts in the Wilderness* which 're-converted' Colin Wilson to Priestley. He was staying at my house at the time and had made some off-handed and derogatory remarks about Priestley. He was delighted to find the essays 'without exception, intelligent and sharply perceptive'. He went on to read *Bright Day* and then was caught. He had, before then, reached the stage where he saw Priestley as 'some kind of confidence man ... Slippery Jack, determined to be all things to all men ...' He read through a dozen or so of Priestley's novels and plays. He found 'a feeling of stunning talent – a profusion of energy and observation and invention that made me envious ... Priestley belongs to the great tradition of the English novel that has come down from Smollett, through Dickens, Trollope, George Meredith and Thomas Hardy to Arnold Bennett and Galsworthy. He has something of Dickens's awesome vitality.' Wilson has his reservations: 'If he does know about the darker side of human nature – people like Dostoevsky's Raskolnikov – he doesn't let on ...' And he maintains that 'the "technical know-how" that enables him to turn problems into plays – *The Linden Tree, An Inspector Calls, They Came to a City* – tends to get in the way of what he is really saying'. But Wilson admits that in the end this really doesn't matter, that

in the best of the plays you feel that he is making a real attempt to grasp human life as a whole to make some comment on it ... He is a poet: he is fascinated by those curious flashes of 'magic' that transform our consciousness, with the idealism of which human beings are capable and the dreary materialism which dictates most of their actions ... He is often a clumsy blunderer but at his clumsiest he is usually saying something so important that it is worth reading him several times to find out what it is. He is a sort of child, endlessly curious about life, and asking the same naïve, direct questions that a child asks ...

There was a new generation and it was still enchanted by him, as its fathers had been. Priestley had never wasted his breath trying to keep up with the *zeitgeist*; but he had always been of the time he was living in, always fully involved in it, he had never dated. No dust had gathered on his magic, as Ion Trewin, another of Colin Wilson's generation and Literary Editor of *The Times*, was to discover:

I first came to Priestley's work at school. I was 16 then and very keen on films. I saw the film version of *The Good Companions* and didn't think much of the film but enjoyed the story. So I read the book and enjoyed it enormously. It seemed so much bigger in spirit than any other modern novel I'd ever come across. Then at about 17 I saw his Time plays on BBC TV. They were a revelation to me. At that age the ideas behind them were completely novel to me. And before I'd only really been exposed to drama with a simple narrative line. The play of ideas was different from what I'd been used to: it made me aware of what can be achieved by the drama. There was, I should add, a period when I felt that Priestley was *démodé*. I was 18 then, a journalist in Plymouth, mostly covering amateur drama. I fell in with an *avant-garde* set who felt that the theatre had a long way to go. Priestley disappeared from my consciousness ... But I remember seeing an amateur production of *Johnson Over Jordan* at this time, and almost against my will finding myself moved by it. I mentioned it to my father [J. C. Trewin, the dramatic critic] and he showed me the original reviews. And I pictured the Basil Dean production with Ralph Richardson as Johnson and was moved again ... There followed a period in my life when I didn't seem to see his plays and I didn't read many novels. But I read *Lost Empires* because of the theatrical background and found that not only was this marvellously evocative but that it was a superb story. That's when I really came back to Priestley. And the vigour and the truth of the sex in it really surprised me – for at my age he seemed as old as Methuselah ... I saw the revival of *An Inspector Calls* at the Mermaid about five years ago. I saw it for the first time – I hadn't seen the film. It was a shock and a revelation. It was full of surprises. I was absolutely riveted. The ending was the biggest surprise of all – most powerful. It came to me absolutely fresh. It hadn't dated at all. In every way it seemed to have worked, it wasn't *passé* ... And I found its genuine moral earnestness, its explicit support of the ... of responsibility for each other, most refreshing. *When We Are Married* I enjoyed in a different way. I admired the skill with which it was put together. It's essentially a homely, undemanding play. But in the production I saw Fred Emney was the drunken photographer and had been allowed to take over, which rather spoilt the balance of the play. But this is the trouble with the theatre. There's only one version of a book but there

are as many versions of a play as there are productions – or even performances. I see him in relation to the drama of the 20th century as in one way
to be bracketed with Noel Coward. He's prolific, his plays *work*, they
generally have only one set and a reasonable size of cast and the right balance
of the sexes. He's practical, he's a man of the theatre. But in another sense
he can justly be compared with Brecht, he goes as deep. I don't suppose
that many critics will accept this, for they make the mistake of valuing
a writer according to his themes. Brecht dealt with big themes, the world
was his province, he was German, therefore he was a big writer. Priestley
deals with people, with individuals, his themes are personal and he's very
English. So he can't be a big writer. But when one thinks about it clearly,
when one realises what his plays *really* are about, then one perceives that
he's just as big as Brecht, that his themes have a huge sweep and grandeur.

And a huge sweep and grandeur are exactly the qualities of his
Literature and Western Man (1960), the result, according to him later,
of passing 'hours and hours with pipe tobacco and desultory reading'.
It is in fact the result of a lifetime's voracious and intensive reading,
an almost inhumanly retentive memory, a capacity for organization
of the highest order and, above all, the strength to carry a workload
that would break many a younger man. It is not, as Priestley says,
a literary history:

The final emphasis here, as the title suggests, is not on Literature but on
Western Man. I have never had in mind a purely literary study; but if a
twenty-volume history of Western Man were being issued, then this might
be the volume devoted to his literature; and indeed, throughout, I think
I have had a vague notion of a sort of composite Western Man, to whom
everything has been related. The appalling business of deciding which
writers should not be merely mentioned but given some critical consideration, decisions that could not be made on any national basis, has had to
be settled from the standpoint of this Western Man ... I have also tried
to keep in mind the sort of people who might be best served by a study
of this kind ... chiefly the considerable numbers of people, in many different countries, who are sufficiently intelligent and sensitive to enjoy most
good literature but are, for various good reasons, rather wary of it, especially the literature of our own age to which I have devoted the largest section
of this book.

Here Priestley makes his declaration of faith in literature and in the traditional values of the West. His purpose is serious, for nothing can be more serious than survival. He doesn't write down, he doesn't trivialize, again and again he emphasizes the fact that the purpose of great literature is to enable us not to pass our time but to use our time, to be explorers of eternity. Literature is not a parlour game. But neither is it the preserve of a small elite. In the section on Tolstoy it is all summed up: '... art should be religious in origin and feeling and ought to be widely understood and appreciated, not the possession of a few, but enjoyed by the mass of people'.

Essentially *Literature and Western Man* is interpretative and not analytical. It is to be regarded in the same light as a novel or a poem. It goes far beyond criticism. The authors Priestley writes about have not been selected to illustrate a theme; the theme arises spontaneously from all that Priestley has read, as a painting arises from the artist's response to a ship or a tree or a hawk or a horse or a girl's face. Art, like sex, is a very serious business – but if there is no delight there is no sex. *Literature and Western Man* is a very serious book; but one reads it in the first place for pleasure.

There was no question in any case of Priestley's creative flow even diminishing. The ideas continued to beckon him, new challenges presented themselves and were accepted. In 1961 for example he published the thriller *Saturn Over the Water*, the light-hearted fantasy *The Thirty-First of June* and – it deserves the special term – a celebration of Charles Dickens. In 1962 there came another thriller, *The Shapes of Sleep*, and his autobiography *Margin Released*.

What is significant about the thrillers – and indeed about all his excursions into this *genre* – is that though they are splendidly ingenious, though their pace never slackens, though they carry the reader irresistibly along to a satisfyingly neat and wholesomely happy ending, they never for one moment frighten us. What is present in even a run-of-the-mill American thriller – sudden death, violence, pain, evil, corruption – simply isn't there. But we needn't turn to American novels for an example: in *Treasure Island* we are frightened, the blind beggar Pew is a creation of genuine evil, and when Long John Silver says 'them that dies will be the lucky ones' he isn't speaking just for effect. Yet Stevenson's experience had included nothing even remotely to compare with Priestley's four years as a front-line soldier. And even those American thriller writers who have had battle experience have had no more than he. Yet only in his second novel *Benighted* is there any reflection of his war experiences, any real terror, any real blood spilled. About this side of life he is as prudish as the Victorians were about sex. The solution to this mystery is indicated by his friend Diana Collins: 'I've never heard Jack say anything really unkind about anybody. He can't bear human pain and he'd never inflict pain ... Jack's really no good at villains. He does believe that there's an active principle of evil in the world, and yet he can't bear to create a really evil character.'

I remember now with amusement and affection the note he sent to me with *Margin Released*. In it he wrote with a certain gloomy relish of 'the night coming, when no man may work'. What actually was coming was a continued creativity. The immediate manifestation of this creativity was the dramatization with Iris Murdoch of her novel *A Severed Head*, which was to run for two years in the West End. Of their collaboration Iris Murdoch says:

I met Jack some time in the 1950s on a BBC programme and adored him at once. What a man, what a character, what an appetite for life! And I adored Jacquetta too – I'd never before met anyone so beautiful and regal. They really are king and queen figures! Yet Jack is also Falstaff – I always think of him as expressed by his own essay on Sir John. About *A Severed Head* – I had already written a play based on the novel, but it was somehow no good and I set it aside. Then things happened very fast, I can't exactly remember how. I recall being in Jack's apartments in the Albany with Jack and a bottle of whisky and laughing a great deal. We wrote the thing in no time at all, and of course Jack's great theatre wisdom solved all the problems and the process taught me a lot about plays and play writing. Jack was the *essential* partner, and could not have been a nicer one. He is a rational and a good man and exceedingly generous, and all deep benevolence. Not just a humane man but a powerfully benevolent one, while being a 'bonny fighter' too. Apart from all this, what a wonderfully shrewd *political* critic he has been over such a long time. He is not only a vastly talented and *exceptionally* versatile and wise writer, he is also such a remarkable human being. And such an *Englishman*! I love him very much.

And there was the entrance of a new element into his work – the realistic treatment of sex. By realistic I specifically don't mean clinical. The line is set where normal good taste sets it. The guide-line is aesthetic rather than moral. Over-explicit physiological detail is worse than immoral, it is boring and untrue: there is more to us than bodies. The bedroom is entered, and even the bath; but we stay away from the bidet and the wc. And what is acknowledged now in Priestley's novels is not only that the hero may sleep with the woman he loves before marriage, but also that he may sleep with a woman he doesn't love, that, whilst not being a cold-hearted sen-sualist, he may love more than one woman.

In *Lost Empires* (1965) the hero, Richard Herncastle, is the assistant of his Uncle Nick, an illusionist. The setting is the music-halls of 1913–14. Once again Priestley is in what I shall term the area of pri-mal experience; Antaneus has both feet on the ground. One uses the word experience in the novelist's sense, not in the sense of direct personal experience. Priestley of course had not been an illusionist's assistant. But he had been in the music-hall audiences, he had glimpsed the performers outside the music-hall – larger than life, gar-ish, outrageous, smelling of cigars and brandy and eau-de-cologne, creatures from another world. And from later experience he was to know the legitimate theatre through and through. The legitimate theatre isn't the same world as the world of the music-hall, but it's closely related to it. Again, being a true novelist, he saved the subject for his maturity.

But this is inaccurate. The music-halls of 1913 to 1914 aren't the subject of the novel. That would be to make it a documentary. The music-halls are here, they are authentic. They were already dying on the eve of the First World War.

'You know,' Richard Herncastle's wife Nancy says, 'everybody thinks of the old music halls being so gay and jolly, hearts of gold everywhere, all what-is-it – gusto and wonderful talent, audiences laughing and crying their heads off – even Meg believes all that – and the last time I read what Dick had written, I could see he hadn't made it like that at all, and that may have been partly my doing, and people don't like having their illusions disturbed –' She stopped to take a long breath. 'I put down as best I could exactly what I saw and thought and felt,' said Herncastle carefully to both of us. 'My belief is that by 1913, when it was organised like big business, the variety stage was already well on the decline. It wasn't any longer a kind of explosion of popular talent. That was already going into films ...'

And this adds another dimension to the story, another sadness. The music-halls are doomed, as the pre-war England was doomed. Priestley looks not only inwards at his characters, but outwards, towards the great events which were to shape their lives, outwards at history.

And in Julie Blane he creates a character who is much more than the conventional Older Woman, the temptress, the Woman with a Past. One sees her not only through the eyes of an eighteen-year-old youth but as she actually was. Her sensuality is real, and so is the sense that she is bad luck for herself and everyone around her. She is the stage partner – or rather stooge – of Tommy Beamish, a brilliant comedian whom the bottle and his private devils are already pulling down into madness. Julie lives with him, he's obsessively jealous of her, but she has no sexual satisfaction from the relationship. She has been on the legitimate stage, she has real talent but she has a problem with the bottle too. Beamish is her last resort and not her choice. As an artist she is capable of better things than being a comedian's stooge; as a woman with strong sexual appetitites, she needs, quite simply, a man.

And Nancy, a blonde of eighteen with 'a saucy look and manner, and legs that were both ravishing and witty', is the girl, 'so pert and saucy and yet somehow so innocent', with whom Richard falls genuinely in love. Nancy is an accomplished singer and dancer but, unlike Julie, she is not truly of the theatre; she enjoys what she's doing but when she's married she'll give it up without a qualm. Furthermore, Nancy is a virgin and, like most girls then and a surprisingly large number today, will remain a virgin until she's married.

Richard loses Nancy, but later in a transit camp in Surrey he is to find her again. There will be a happy ending. But before he loses her Julie becomes his mistress. He loves Nancy. Nancy is the right woman for him. And Nancy is eighteen and Julie is thirty-five. He is warned against Julie by the Russian landlady of a theatrical boarding-house:

'Deek, I speak with you as mother – about loafe –'

145

'Loaf?' But then I realised she meant love.

'Between man and woman loafe is good. Between girl and boy, like you, loafe is good. Between boy and woman – no real true loafe. It is 'unger for sex, this kind of loafe. All there is between you, Deek, and Mees Blane, is 'unger for sex, animal feeling. No, follish to deny. We have seen. We have already spoken of it. We *know*. With you, Deek, is because you are yong, strong man. You want girl. You have no girl. With this Mees Blane, it is not the same. She is mature woman, very strong in sex, anyone can see, and she has terrible 'unger.'

He doesn't take any notice. He knows that what his landlady says is true, he knows that he loves Nancy. He knows that he risks losing Nancy. The strength of the writing here is that on the one hand we acknowledge his landlady's wisdom but on the other we know that her words of wisdom will fall upon deaf ears:

It was exactly six-and-a-half minutes, by my new watch, when I tapped on the door of my room with the whisky bottle, out of which I'd already had a nip, and then walked in, not quite knowing what to expect. She was standing there completely naked ... I took in her beauty as I might have done that of a landscape or a noble picture, outside desire, without wanting to possess her. Nowadays we live in a world of nudes and semi-nudes, of tanned arms and shoulders, calves and thighs, so often exposed and browned that their skin seems like a kind of clothing; but then, when women were covered from top to toe, a nakedness like this was an extraordinary revelation, as if a living statue, pearly, opalescent, faintly glowing, had miraculously stepped out of the dark huddle of clothes...

And afterwards there is the reaction. He has made it, he's joined the club, he is a man, he's been fully initiated. He is triumphant, he's strutting round the arena acknowledging the applause. He's no longer a timid ignorant boy. He knows it all. This is genuine, this is in character, this is the feeling which most men remember. But what is also genuine is that he feels also 'a huge vague sadness'. The sadness here is as real as the sex. And what is real too is the 'exultation of the predatory young male'. There are several people here within one skull. The whole complexity of the sexual act is revealed. There is the artist there too, the memory of the beauty of Julie's body – outside sex, outside morality, outside even Dick himself. And looking at it now, twelve years after publication, I once again realize that

I can bring to mind few other living novelists who can write as well about sex, who realize that more is involved in the act of love than two bodies.

But after this in 1968 followed his longest novel, 300,000 words, *The Image Men*, which he describes as 'my first favourite among all my novels'. It's easy to see why. In the first instance, there is its sheer length. There is a common illusion that to write a novel of 300,000 words is no more difficult than to write a novel of 100,000 words, that it simply takes three times as long. The fact is that it not only takes three times as long but is much more – as far as one can be quantitative about these matters – than three times as difficult. With a long novel an incomparably greater richness of texture and an incomparably greater complexity of narrative can be achieved. There is a more vivid sense of the immense spectacle of life itself, of what Priestley once described to me as 'the whole marvellous *tangle* of things'. The form comes into its own, it's used to the fullest stretch, there's no aspect of life it can't contain. Above all, without being sociology, it can present the reader with the true likeness of a society and the forces which shape that society. But the sheer technical problems are immense. Quite simply, there are more characters to handle, more threads to the narrative, more for the author to carry in his head. And the original impetus must always be maintained, there must be a continuing narrative zest.

To summarize the story it's enough to say that its heroes, Professor Cosmo Saltana and Dr Owen Tuby, begin their adventures flat-broke in a Bayswater hotel, and end them happy, in love and with £50,000 and £42,000 in their pockets respectively. The source of their good fortune is the Institute of Social Imagistics, invented out of necessity and a few double whiskies by Saltana. In its first manifestation it is sociological and has its trial run in the new University of Brockshire; in its second manifestation it is a resoundingly successful public relations firm. The book was well received and, miraculously, was seen exactly as what it was – 'delicious social satire, penetrating sharply the pomposities of both the academic and commercial shenanigans', to quote *The Bookman*. The point has been made that Saltana and Tuby wouldn't have had so easy a time of it in real life, that the commercial world in general and the political world in particular is much tougher than Priestley supposes. And men as clever as Saltana and Tuby would never have been flat-broke in a Bayswater hotel but long since landed themselves tax-free sinecures with Unesco or the Common Market. And personally I feel that middle-aged men who drink and smoke and eat as much as Saltana and Tuby would not be quite such tigers in bed as they're made out to be. But this is to break the butterfly on the wheel. For it is a butterfly, a *jeu d'ésprit*, but on a scale that no other writer would even dare to contemplate.

And still the night had not come. It still was not enough to write in his seventies an enormously long satirical novel in which the original inspiration was sustained from start to finish. There followed in 1969 *The Prince of Pleasure and His Regency*, in 1970 *The Edwardians* and in 1972 *Victoria's Heyday*. These were coffee-table books, a term which generally carries undertones of disparagement. They were written for the general public, not for the scholar, their format was necessarily large, the illustrations were a vital complement to the text, not dispensable luxuries. But as Priestley points out, 'these were far from being hack jobs'. He selected the illustrations and, just as the texts were the fruits of a lifetime's reading and an unfettered mind, so were the illustrations the fruits of a lifetime's looking at pictures – and, indeed everything of delight in the visual world – and an unfettered eye. The books weren't meant to be the last word on their subjects but to introduce the reader to their subjects and to induce them to carry on further for themselves. They are the work of a young enthusiast, they are a sharing of his delight. And they are full of fresh insights: I know personally that until I read *The Prince of Pleasure and His Regency* I had not fully realized exactly how great the Prince Regent's potentialities were. I had not realized that, despite his fatal weaknesses, he was a humane and cultivated man. I had not seen him as he really was, lazy and sensual and fallible, but always in his imperfect way on the side of the angels. Looked at in one way, these three works are diversions – diversions for Priestley too, a change of pace from novels and plays. But, looked at in another way, they made their readers think, and take pleasure in thinking. They are the kind of books of which his father, the headmaster, would have been particularly proud.

And in 1972 he published *Over the Long High Wall*. This was a short book, the quintessence of the thoughts which had never been far from his mind since he had first come to grips with the question of Time in the Arizona desert. He once said to Norman Collins: 'Do you know what I really want to do? I want to fill a big gap. There's no popular introduction to philosophy, which, after all, is about the only really important question – what life's all about.' And now in his seventy-eighth year he was attempting to answer the question of what life's all about. His main argument is that today our society isn't even thinking about that question, that its thinking is purely in materialistic terms, that anything which won't fit into these terms, it won't even consider. It isn't, one need hardly say, a call to religion, the record of a man finding God. (Though he might well have pointed out that organized religion, even when most stultified and formal, does at least acknowledge the existence of a mystery.) What he sees is

the world lying in the shadow of the long high wall, the passing-time wall, which we have imagined into existence as our beliefs have shrunk and hardened, emptying the universe of higher levels of being and all far-flung adventures of the spirit, and refusing to accept the one magical gift we possess – our consciousness.

It is an important book, possibly the most important of all his books. Though it is never less than supremely clear and concise, its literary merit is irrelevant. It is important because, when one comes to think of it, even the churches now are more and more turning away from the question of why we are here, refusing to consider the vertical relationship of man with God, and more concentrating upon the horizontal relationship of man with man. At the very least – and this Priestley would have been prepared for, even welcomed – there should have been a storm of condemnation. Instead, as he bitterly remarked: 'It came out to receive the kiss of death ... I regard this book as the supreme flop of my career in publishing.'

He was not silenced, he did not sulk in his tent. *Outcries and Asides*, a collection of some two hundred short informal pieces, published in 1974, shows no evidence of failing powers or of defeat of spirit. This is a volume of table talk, relaxed, witty, wise, ultimately generous and serene. There's no trace of snappiness or disjointedness, the book adds up to a whole, he is our host at a long dinner-party which is never for one moment too long. And in the same year there was a travel book, *A Visit to New Zealand*, illustrated with reproductions of New Zealand painters and his own gouaches.

(There was also reported in August 1974 a new play, *Time Was, Time Is*, on the Time theme with two acts and a cast of fourteen, going back to 1914, employing double sets and double costumes. A West End management was interested, but the project, the theatre being what it is, was stillborn and sadly the play, his first new one for twenty years, can only be mentioned in passing.)

A Visit to New Zealand is – as far as one dare predict – the record of the last of his travels. It's a pleasant book, a happy book, his eye is as sharp as ever, his memory as keen, he captures the essence of the country, its newness, its freshness, its hopefulness, its contented but not complacent isolation from the rest of the world. But the autumnal note is there. He was reaching the age when he would not want or be able to go very far from home. Still the creative flow continued. In 1975 there was *Particular Pleasures*: appreciations of paintings, music, actors and comedians, and *The Carfitt Crisis*. In the same year the adaptation of *The Good Companions*, revised by Ronald Harwood, was produced at the Albery Theatre.

Judi Dench, who played the part of Miss Trant, says:

The story of *The Good Companions* was wonderful – Ronnie Harwood adapted it and he did a wonderful job. It contained the whole essence of that period, it looked absolutely right, the people who saw it absolutely loved it. It ran for eight months, and I'm sure that it could have run for longer. I'm sure that what killed it was the IRA bomb scare . . . people naturally were nervous about coming to the West End . . . But I really did love doing it and Michael my husband saw it nine times and enjoyed it each time.

What I'm sad about is that I've never been in any of his other plays – he writes marvellous parts for women. I'm particularly thinking of *The Linden Tree* which I saw with Andrew Cruikshank and Maggie Tyzack – it's a superb play, it's really warm and tender.

I've really met two J. B. Priestleys. The first one came to a rehearsal and we were all paralysed with fright. He looked at me and I'm sure that he didn't see me as his idea of Miss Trant. Though later he saw me in my stage costume with my Marcel wave wig and then he did approve of me.

The second J. B. Priestley invited us to lunch at his home in Stratford. He wasn't a bit frightening then, and he was in very good form. The time passed like a flash, he was enormously entertaining. I remember that in one of the windows there was a big carved fish eye which seemed to have a magnifying effect. He went out into the garden and we saw his face through the fish eye beckoning us, and at that moment I saw him as an enchanter, a real magician.

Looking back I sense about him a feeling not of sadness exactly but as if he were looking for something which he hadn't found. He's written so much, achieved so much, but I feel that there's still more he wants to write, still more he wants to achieve. And yet that's not quite what I want to say. Perhaps it's enough to say that he's searching for some kind of perfection and there'll always be a further perfection beyond it. After all, that's what art is about ...

In 1976 there was the revised *English Humour* and a 36,000-word novella, *Found, Lost, Found – or The English Way of Life*. In his old age he was still more productive than most writers in their youth. The novella is light-hearted; it was short, one feels, because 36,000 words was its proper length, because the novella is a form in its own right, a form he enjoyed trying his hand at. The hero, a clever but lazy young man, is drifting into a sort of emotional limbo, aided by gin, when he meets a bright and loving and giving girl who, he senses, will take him back into the mainstream again. But she doesn't want to make things too easy for him, she wants him to prove himself: she disappears and sets him the task of finding her. The happy ending will be when he finds her.

Priestley, who in some ways is curiously naïve, told me that he thought there was the material for a good TV serial there. Indeed there is; and it would be just what the majority of viewers like. But the decision-makers in TV, though not as lunatic as their counterparts in the theatre, have for the most part a positive prejudice against giving the viewer what they like. Priestley would in fact have had a great deal to give to the TV medium, and had the decision-makers in TV been rational or even whole-heartedly commercial, they should have been clamouring for original TV material from him right from the very start. The medium would have been all the more attractive to him since, unlike the cinema, it is still very much a writer's medium. These are vain regrets, occasioned by the fact that whilst writing this book I've been working happily in TV with a small company and have for the first time realized the potential of the medium and, coming back to the book, have realized how much Priestley would have enjoyed it too.

However, he need have no regrets. If there is anything which he hasn't done which he could have done, it isn't because of laziness or of timidity at trying something new, but for reasons beyond his control. When allowed into the arena, he has always won; it isn't his fault that certain arenas locked their gates against him. It doesn't matter, because he's done his work and his work is alive. There has been nothing new from him since the autobiographical volume, *Instead of the Trees*, in 1976 – a gap of some two years, the longest ever – and it seems now as if indeed the long night is coming. 'I used to believe that the subconscious – where all the creation is done – couldn't age,' he said recently to Diana Collins. 'I think now that I was wrong.' And certainly *Instead of the Trees* does have a genuine valedictory note. He counts his blessings, past and present (and he acknowledges how much more he has had to count than most men), he remembers with delight and gratitude all that he has been and all that he has seen. *Instead of the Trees*, though it records relentlessly the disabilities of old age, when the most commonplace activities like dressing become an increasingly irksome burden, is not an unhappy or despairing book, it is in no way to be compared with a sustained outpouring of rage and hopelessness like H. G. Wells's *Mind at the End of Its Tether*, for what Wells did was to admit defeat, to give up fighting ... And there is no pain, physical or mental, no misfortune or combination of misfortunes, which could make Priestley give up fighting. He will not resign himself, he will not become the amiable old codger nodding in the inglenook, he refuses, as he himself says, to go gentle into that good night. He still doesn't quite believe that he is old (though in his teens he frequently wrote of himself as if middle-aged, in his middle age as if he were old, and on the verge of old age as if the undertaker were already measuring him up). He says: 'There is still in me a younger man, trapped, struggling to get out.'

Meeting him recently, I found this easy to believe. It's as it was the first time I met him in 1957. The camera – and particularly the television camera – is a liar. In the flesh he seems a good twenty years younger than in his photographs. There is somewhere in his face a strange indestructible youthfulness. He perhaps walks more slowly than he did, but that slowness isn't painful, it seems slowness through choice, not necessity. And his mind is as active as ever, his eyes and his ears are in working order, one has never – and this is the great joy of being in his company – felt sorry for him. He has his beautiful home – and another pleasure of being in his company is to be in a genuinely beautiful house, a house in the grand style, about which one can feel that its owner deserves it, has worked for every stone of it. He has his children, his grandchildren, a great circle of friends – diminished by death now, but so great that never will he be without friends to warm him – and he has, beyond the great circle of personal friends, all those who know and love his work and so know and love him. He will continue to grumble at stupidity and inefficiency, at bureaucracy and government, against all that makes life irksome for the minority like him and – which is always forgotten – almost unendurable for the majority. Most of his grumbling has been not on behalf of himself but on behalf of others less fortunate.

Above all, he has had for nearly a quarter of a century a wife who is like another self, who is genuinely his other half, a wife whom he never tires of talking with, but a wife with whom he could sit quite contentedly in silence, glad to be with her. He has had everything: and he has given everything too. To be with him is still a pleasure. There is still the pleasure of hero-worship, but above that there is the fact that he still exudes energy and warmth, that he doesn't rob one of energy, that there is never any sense of calculation or of malice. It is doubtful if he would recognize that feeling, any more than he would recognize envy. He told me once that he didn't want to be ninety. 'When you're ninety,' he said, 'another man takes over. You're not *you*, you're this other man. I saw this happen to Shaw.'

I don't doubt that it happened to Shaw, because Shaw was always

a cold man, generating light but not heat, seriously approving elimi-
nation – which is to say mass murder – of those he termed undesirable
social types. The other man had always been lurking inside Shaw.
He was never even near Priestley. Priestley has always had plenty
of ideas, has always loved to make glittering new theories, but those
ideas have always been based upon human realities. Theories for him
have been to serve human beings, not human beings to serve theories.
There is no theory that he would think worth a single innocent life.
He is on the side of life, of the life within every individual, not of
the life-force.

It is for other people – who may or may not have plenty of evidence
– to decide if I am life-enhancing. But I will add this. There may have
been too much fault-finding, rumbling grumbling, loud denouncing of
this, that and the other; but at least I have never been one of the huge,
dim, conformist or apathetic multitude, advertisers' fodder, politicians'
gulls, media mugs, all of them life-defeating, more than half-entangled in
the death-wish. But then if I didn't think we now have too many of these
types, I might not be a pessimist. And I am – and I enjoy it. So – quite
possibly – life-enhancing.

He will always march towards the sound of the guns. He is more
than a man, he is an army, *our* army, an army of volunteers. I don't
believe it when he tells me now that he'll write no more – retirement
is for ordinary men, not for him. I don't believe, to use Colin Wilson's words, that his endless curiosity is now ending, that he'll ever
stop asking questions. In October 1977 he accepted the Order of
Merit; he was right to do so, because this is the highest of honours,
with a strictly limited number of recipients. (He has himself described
it as 'an Order of Merit that really was – and still is – an order of
merit, not just another title and ribbon to reward contributors to
party funds or to compensate politicians kicked out of the Cabinet'.)
In a radio interview he said, typically: 'I've only two things to say
about it. First, I deserve it. Second, they've been too long about giving
me it. There'll be another vacancy very soon.' But he was actually
delighted to be awarded it; he has refused other honours, this being
the only one he has ever desired. He isn't and never will be a Grand
Old Man, a totem figure, a symbol, an idol. In the narrow sense
of the word he is old, and in the narrow sense of the word he will

die. But what dies, to adapt the epitaph of Hodson of Hodson's Horse, will only be all of him that can die. What can't die will be with us as long as the language, will nourish future generations as it has nourished mine: *Priestley lives.*

Selected Works

The dates for his plays, filmscripts, and opera libretto are those of first performance unless otherwise indicated. Novels, essays, etc., are shown under the date of first publication.

1918 *The Chapman of Rhymes* (verse)

1922 *Brief Diversions* (miscellany)
      Papers from Lilliput (sketches)

1923 *I for One* (essays)

1924 *Figures in Modern Literature*
      (criticism)

1925 *The English Comic Characters*
      (criticism)

1926 *George Meredith* (criticism)
      Talking (essays)

1927 *Adam in Moonshine* (novel)
      Open House (essays)
      Thomas Love Peacock (criticism)
      Benighted (novel)
      The English Novel (criticism)

1928 *Apes and Angels* (essays)

1929 *The Good Companions* (novel),
      dramatized with Edward
      Knoblock, 1931
      English Humour (criticism)
      The Balconinny (essays)
      Farthing Hall (fiction)

1930 *The Town Mayor of Miraucourt*
      (short story)
      Angel Pavement (novel)

1932 *Self-Selected Essays*
      Dangerous Corner (play)
      Faraway (novel)

1933 *Wonder Hero* (novel)
      The Roundabout (play) (date
      published)
      Laburnum Grove (play)

1934 *English Journey* (travel/social
      criticism)
      Eden End (play)

1935 *Duet in Floodlight* (play)
      Cornelius (play)

1936 *Spring Tide* (play) under the
      pseudonym Peter Goldsmith,
      with George Billam
      Bees on the Boatdeck (play)
      They Walk in the City (novel)

1937 *Midnight on the Desert*
      (autobiography)
      Time and the Conways (play)
      I Have Been Here Before (play)

People at Sea (play)
Music at Night (play)

1938 *The Doomsday Men* (novel)
When We Are Married (play)
Mystery at Greenfingers (play)

1939 *Johnson Over Jordan* (play)
Rain upon Godshill
(autobiography)
Let the People Sing (novel)

1940 *Postscripts* (broadcast talks)

1941 *Out of the People* (commentary)

1942 *Goodnight, Children* (play)
Black-Out in Gretley (story)

1943 *They Came to a City* (play)
Daylight on Saturday (novel)
The Man-Power Story
(commentary)
British Women go to War
(sociology)

1944 *Desert Highway* (play)
How Are They At Home? (play)

1945 *Three Men in New Suits* (novel)
The Long Mirror (play)

1946 *An Inspector Calls* (play)
Jenny Villiers (play)
The Secret Dream (essay)
Bright Day (novel)

1947 *The Arts under Socialism* (lecture)
Theatre Outlook (criticism)
Ever Since Paradise (play)
The Linden Tree (play)
The Rose and Crown (play) (date
published)

1948 *Home is Tomorrow* (play)
The Golden Fleece (play)

1949 *The Olympians* (opera libretto)
Delights (essays)
Summer Day's Dream (play)

1950 *Last Holiday* (filmscript)
Bright Shadow (play)

1951 *Festival at Farbridge* (novel)

1952 *Dragon's Mouth* (play) with
Jacquetta Hawkes
Treasure on Pelican (play)

1953 *The Other Place* (stories)
Private Rooms (one-act play)
(date published)
Try It Again (one-act play) (date
published)
Mother's Day (one-act play)
(date published)

1954 *The Magicians* (novel)
Low Notes on a High Level
(fiction)
The White Countess (play) with
Jacquetta Hawkes

1955 *Mr Kettle and Mrs Moon* (play)
Journey Down a Rainbow (travel)
with Jacquetta Hawkes
The Golden Entry (play) (date
published)

1956 *These Our Actors* (play) (date
published)

1957 *The Glass Cage* (play)
Thoughts in the Wilderness (essay)
The Art of the Dramatist (essay)

1958 *Topside, or the Future of England*
(essay)

1960 *Literature and Western Man*
(criticism)

1961 *Saturn Over the Water* (novel)
*Charles Dickens: A Pictorial
Biography*
The Thirty-First of June (novel)

1962 *The Shapes of Sleep* (novel)
Margin Released (literary
reminiscences)

1963 *A Severed Head* (play) with Iris
      Murdoch
      The Pavilion of Masks (play)
      (date published)

1964 *Sir Michael and Sir George*
      (novel)
      Man and Time (essay)

1965 *Lost Empires* (novel)

1966 *The Moment and Other Pieces*
      (essays)
      Salt is Leaving (novel)

1967 *It's an Old Country* (novel)

1968 *The Image Men* (novel, vol. 1):
      Out of Town

1969 *The Image Men* (novel, vol. 2):
      London End
      Essays of Five Decades, ed. Susan
      Cooper

      *The Prince of Pleasure and his
      Regency* (social history)

1970 *The Edwardians* (social history)

1971 *Snoggle* (children's fiction)

1972 *Victoria's Heyday* (social history)
      Over the Long High Wall (essay)

1973 *The English* (social history)

1974 *Outcries and Asides* (essays)
      A Visit to New Zealand (travel)

1975 *The Carfitt Crisis* (short stories)
      Particular Pleasures (essays)
      English Humour (essay)

1976 *Found, Lost, Found – or The
      English Way of Life* (novella)

1977 *Instead of the Trees*
      (autobiography)

Index

INDEX